Teacher appraisal

Appraisal and staff development form an integral part of the range of accountability measures now operating in schools. In this book, Cyril and Doreen Poster look at the purpose of appraisal, and its importance within the context of the 'school effectiveness' movement. They stress that the central concern must be the personal and professional development of teachers. Appraisal should help teachers to assess their own performance, thereby enabling them to raise standards in school and classroom.

The book covers the introduction of appraisal in England and Wales, drawing comparisons with appraisal in the USA and in tertiary education. It deals in detail with classroom performance, goalsetting, the appraisal interview, interviewing skills, headteacher appraisal, the appraisal of managerial skills and the role in appraisal of governors and advisers. While the book is not a training manual, it does contain valuable training material, case studies and questionnaires, all presented against the background of a cohesive educational philosophy.

Cyril and Doreen Poster are experienced educators and trainers, and have worked for the past four years as consultants to LEAs organising their training for appraisal, and running workshops for education officers, advisers, inspectors and primary and secondary teachers.

EDUCATIONAL MANAGEMENT SERIES
Edited by Cyril Poster

Teacher appraisal

A guide to training

Cyril and Doreen Poster
with Maurice Benington

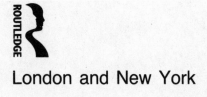

London and New York

First published 1991
by Routledge
11 New Fetter Lane, London EC4P 4EE

Simultaneously published in the USA and Canada
by Routledge
a division of Routledge, Chapman and Hall, Inc.
29 West 35th Street, New York, NY 10001

Typeset in Garamond by Columns
Printed and bound in Great Britain by Biddles Ltd,
Guildford and King's Lynn

British Library Cataloguing in Publication Data
 Teacher appraisal : a guide to training.
 I. Great Britain. Schools. Teachers. Performance. Assessment
 I. Title II. Poster, Doreen *1923–* III. Benington, Maurice
 371.1440941

ISBN 0–415–06167–9
ISBN 0–415–06168–7 pbk

Library of Congress Cataloging-in-Publication Data
has been applied for

Contents

Figures

Training materials

Introduction

In 1986, having between us worked in every field of education from pre-school to higher, and at every level from classroom teacher to principal and senior research fellow, we decided to become self-employed trainers. We did not at that time anticipate that by far the greatest part of our work would rapidly become training for appraisal and staff development.

In four years we have, we estimate, run workshops for well over two thousand teachers, advisers, inspectors and education officers, ranging from one-day awareness raising sessions to four-day action learning modules spread over several months. We have also acted as consultants to several LEAs as they have formulated their policies for the introduction of appraisal. We make no claim to great expertise; but we do believe that a book about training should have been thoroughly tested 'in the fire', and that is most certainly true of what the reader will find on the following pages.

We have not written a book *about* appraisal. There are a number of such books on the market, including several excellent ones in the Routledge Education Management series. Nor have we set out to write a training manual. Had we done that, we would have doubtless succumbed to two temptations common among those who produce manuals: to be prescriptive, and to dwell on product rather than process. We call this 'a guide to training' in the expectation that it will be useful at all levels from in-house to LEA- and provider-led workshops, and particularly because we believe that the materials that it contains will be valuable only in so far as they can be adapted to local needs and circumstances.

We completed the final revision of the text in the month when the then Secretary of State for Education issued the draft National Framework for appraisal which, by the time this book appears, will almost certainly have been agreed or modified. While we share with LEAs, schools and teacher unions reservations about some aspects of his scheme, above all the paucity of funding provided both for training and for the implementation of appraisal, we nevertheless applaud the fact that LEAs are empowered to decide the pace of innovation and schools to accommodate appraisal to their existing management styles and structures. We see appraisal and staff development as central to the whole range of accountability measures that have been introduced since the mid-1980s and therefore of vital importance in improving performance in the classroom and the status of the profession. Throughout this book we have sought to keep this statement from *Education Observed* in the forefront of our minds:

> The one undisputed requirement of good education is good teaching, and performance in the classroom lies at the heart of the teacher's professional skill and of the standard of learning achieved.
>
> (HMI, 1985a)

Alongside it we would place the following sentences, which seem to us to encapsulate what is vital to good practice:

> The essence of appraisal should be positive. Appraisal should be about 'prizing' and 'valuing' what is seen.
>
> (Montgomery, 1985)

There are many people whom we would like to thank for their assistance with this book. Pride of place must go without question to our co-author, Maurice Benington of Bristol Polytechnic, who wrote most of chapter 4 and who contributed extensively to the opening chapter.

From the USA we have had unstinting help by letter, phone and audiotape from our good friend Shirley Hord of the Southwest Educational Development Laboratory in Austin, Texas; and, through her, the Oklahoma State Department of Education and, in particular, the State Superintendent of Public Instruction, Gerald E. Hoeltzel; the Texas Education Agency of the Texas State Board of Education; Board of Education, Lovington District, New Mexico; Charles Knox, Harry Eskew, Twila Ferris, Maxine Converse and John Connell.

From Dudley LEA: Ian Cleland, Chief Adviser, and Clive Burns, Senior Secondary Adviser; Pearl White, Mary Riley, Phil Lucas, Trevor Taylor, all primary headteachers, who formed the primary appraisal tutor team and whose help in trialling our materials we have much valued; Anna Smith, formerly Director of the GRASP project, now a primary headteacher; Barbara O'Connor, Carol Raphael, Barry Bainbridge, Malcolm Hewitt, secondary headteachers, who worked closely with us in establishing the Dudley secondary schools appraisal training.

From the Regional Staff College, Dudley: Ken Lambert, the Director, a good friend and himself a trainer of distinction; Harry Moore, Harry Chalton and Ian McGuff, Associate Directors.

From Sandwell LEA: Peter Davies, Chief Adviser, with and for whom we planned workshops for advisers and support teachers.

From Bristol University School of Education: Cyril Poster's former colleagues from the National Development Centre for School Management

Training, Ray Bolam, the director, Agnes MacMahon and Mike Wallace; and from the Further Professional Studies Department, Peter Taylor, In-Service Tutor, and Ann Mattock, then Course Administrator.

The DES has kindly granted us permission to reproduce as Appendix 1 the Code of Practice contained in the supplementary guidance to the draft National Framework. It is necessary to state that LEAs are not obliged to adhere to details of the supplementary guidance, but we consider it unlikely that any will wish to depart from a Code of Practice agreed by the profession as a whole.

We are also grateful to Alyson Courtenay of the BBC's Open University Production Centre, to Open University Educational Enterprises and to Focus in Education for their valuable help in the compilation of Appendix 2.

Finally, two personal friends, Hilary Bassett, who contributed to our thinking on the appraisal of early years teachers; and Sue Thorne, who transcribed our transatlantic audiotapes.

We have sought at all times to avoid sexist language in this book. We have done this, not by what we regard as the ugly and tedious use of he/she, but by using sometimes the masculine form and sometimes the feminine for the senior post in any situation we describe in the text. For case studies we have chosen forenames which can be either male or female, in order not to prejudice the discussion or pre-empt the choice of role-player.

All training materials in this book may be photocopied by individual trainers wishing to make use of them in workshops and on courses. In all other respects the conventions of copyright must be observed.

Cyril and Doreen Poster
Bristol

Chapter 1

What is appraisal?

All organisations – hospitals, schools, factories, businesses – exist to provide a service or product. Appraisal is a means of promoting, through the use of certain techniques and procedures, the organisation's ability to accomplish its mission of providing a better service or product while at the same time enhancing staff satisfaction and development. If employees are to perform effectively, they must be well motivated, understand what is expected of them and have the ability and skills to fulfil their responsibilities.

In many organisations an annual review of some kind takes place between staff members and their immediate managers. There is very little conformity over what this review is called: staff appraisal, staff development review, performance appraisal, performance review are among the terms most commonly used. We draw a distinction between two main trends in appraisal: performance appraisal and staff development reviews.

Performance appraisal focuses on setting achievable, often relatively short-term goals and by giving feedback: on task clarification through reaching consensus on an employee's objectives consistent with those of the organisation; and on identifying training needs as indicated either by shortcomings in performance or by potentialities for higher levels of endeavour.

Staff development review focuses, through the identification of individual developmental needs and subsequent training or self-development, on improving the ability of the employees to perform in their present or future roles.

In brief, the former is concerned with the task, the latter with the individual.

This distinction is of course an over-simplification, since the performance of any organisation will depend both on the delivery system and on those who are to deliver it. There may well be an infinite number of variations in the marriage of these two styles, but it is virtually impossible to conceive of an appraisal system that totally ignores the other element.

For simplicity and brevity, we intend to use the word appraisal throughout this book, glossing it only where necessary to make our intention and meaning absolutely clear. Most readers will be well aware that there has been a good deal of antagonism in educational circles to the use of this word: the next chapter, which deals with the history of the introduction of appraisal, explains why. Some local education authorities have fought shy of the word to such an extent that they use the term staff development exclusively, even though it is clear that the system they are considering does not confine itself to this element. Others have used appraisal and staff development, a term which accurately reflects the concerns of administrators and teachers alike, but which is too cumbersome for repeated use.

INDIVIDUAL AND ORGANISATIONAL NEEDS

Appraisal is one of a number of techniques for integrating the individual into the organisation. Each individual comes into an organisation with unique needs and objectives, preferences for ways of doing things and hopes for wide-ranging satisfactions. One may be ambitious, intending to achieve well in a short time and move rapidly up the career ladder. Another may wish no more than to perform competently, to enjoy the social satisfactions of working in a particular organisation and to spend his or her spare time in activities unconnected with the workplace. The problem for individuals is to make their contributions within organisations set up by others in such a way as also to achieve their own goals and to satisfy their own personal and other needs. The problem for the organisation, whether it is a school, an office or a business, is to harness the unique talents of individuals and coordinate their activities towards the achievement of the organisation's objectives by efficient and effective means. This process of matching the needs of individuals and coordinating their activities can best be described as 'integrating the individual and the organisation'.

There are many interactive processes which monitor and control the process of integration of individuals during their time in an organisation and which influence their behaviour. They include

- recruitment, selection, placement, induction;
- training, coaching, delegation;
- reward and payment systems;
- performance reviews, appraisal;
- counselling, grievance and disciplinary procedures;
- exit interviews.

Since it is likely that the interests of the individual and the organisation will not match perfectly, there will be a need to reconcile differences in most of these processes. The methods of handling these differences will vary from one organisation to another: in one the differences will be concealed; in another they will be explored and a satisfactory resolution will be negotiated; in a third the more powerful party, usually the organisation, will impose its solution. The approach to the handling of differences will of course colour the appraisal or other integrating process. Where a negotiating or problem-solving approach is used to handle differences these processes will require give and take on both sides, trust and open communication.

The accomplishment of a task is not only a matter of individual ability and motivation, but very often depends on the support of colleagues. A small team of cooperating individuals working on a common task can usually handle higher levels of stress and maintain confidence and morale in the face of problems and difficulties better than can individuals operating in isolation. Thus, both for the social satisfaction of individuals and for the achievement of objectives, a supportive, cooperative climate within an organisation is desirable.

The needs of individuals have been extensively analysed by occupational psychologists and sociologists. Not surprisingly, it has been found that while the needs differ according to age, culture, personality and social class, there is among middle managers and professionals a fairly common set of wants or needs. These may be listed as a need for responsibility, autonomy, a sense of achievement, interesting and challenging work, opportunities for personal growth and development, and the occasion to use skills (Herzberg, 1966; Vroom, 1964).

In addition to these psychological and social needs and wants, individuals must be provided with essential information if they are to achieve the objectives of the organisation. They need to know:

- what is expected of them, that is, what objectives they should be trying to achieve;
- what are the areas of their responsibilities, authority and discretion;
- whether they are achieving their objectives and otherwise performing as required;
- how they might correct any shortfall between objectives and achievement.

These requirements suggest certain desiderata for any integrating process, including appraisal.

ORGANISATIONAL MANAGEMENT STYLES

Different organisations base their employee relations on very different sets of assumptions. McGregor (1960) posited two polarised sets of assumptions that organisations might have about their workers. These he called Theory X and Theory Y.

A bureaucratic, hierarchical organisation is likely to act as if it assumed that people:

> dislike work, have little ambition, want security and require to be coerced, controlled or threatened with punishment. In contrast, Theory Y holds that staff will seek responsibility if the conditions are appropriate, exercise self-direction and control if they become committed to organisational objectives, and respond to rewards associated with goal-attainment.
>
> (Dennison and Shenton, 1987)

In practice, organisations rarely conform wholly to either polarity. It is now widely accepted that organisational behaviour, while to some extent predetermined by the organisation's self-image, will swing on an arc between these two polarities according to the demands of a given situation and the response of management to those demands. Burns and Stalker (1968) produced such a model in which the terms *mechanistic* and *organic* represent these two polarities. The mechanistic type of organisation is defined as one:

> suitable to stable conditions, to a hierarchical management structure in which there is a clear definition of assigned roles, formal and mainly vertical communication, and a built-in system of checks and supervision. The organic type of organisation, on the other hand, is designed to adapt to a rapid rate of change, to situations in which new and unfamiliar problems continually arise which cannot be broken down and distributed among the existing specialist roles. Relationships are therefore lateral rather than vertical, and form and reform according to the demands of the particular problem.
>
> (Poster, 1976)

The rate of change currently to be met in educational institutions at all levels calls for situational responses which may appear to be demanding now one management style, now another. There can nevertheless be discerned in most organisations an underlying management style. Appraisal helps to make staff more understanding of the need for these variations while at the same time encouraging management to make tempered judgments about the style required in a particular situation and not to bow to whatever wind appears to blow.

ORGANISATIONAL CLIMATE AND APPRAISAL

Organisational climate is a concept that refers to the different cultures or qualities possessed by organisations and is a function of such factors as whether the structure is hierarchical and bureaucratic or informal and dynamic, and whether initiative and risk, or rule-following and conformity are rewarded. Some organisations tend to value and support individual efforts, to encourage cooperation and reward achievement. Others require conformity to rules and procedures and respect for seniors.

The differences in organisational climate will be expressed in the processes used to integrate the individual and the organisation. A hierarchical organisation, for example, is likely to view an induction process as one in which the newcomer is given a grounding in the organisation's ways of doing things. A more dynamic organisation will use induction as an opportunity to demonstrate the breadth of discretion and responsibility offered to the newcomer. Appraisal in one organisation may be concerned with assessing the extent of an individual's conformity to the organisational ethos and with measuring how far he has met targets; in another, with encouraging initiative, self-development and achievement.

It is clear that there may well be a mismatch between the wants of the individual and the climate of the organisation. An organisation may treat its members as if they were lazy, untalented, unmotivated and irresponsible. Yet within that organisation may be individuals who, possessing but being unable to deploy the skills and abilities which the organisation most desperately needs, feel marginalised and unfulfilled. This mismatch becomes highlighted on each occasion the individual makes formal contact with the organisation in any of its procedures, including appraisal, and eventually leads to intense frustration, demotivation, low effectiveness and adaptability, poor morale, low job satisfaction, high staff turnover and the rest of the ills that beset a sick organisation.

We have postulated that appraisal is one of a battery of processes for integrating the individual into the organisation, and that this desired outcome is achieved in part by meeting the psychological and social needs of the individual. We have argued that failure to meet these needs is likely to result in organisational ill-health. However, an organisation which bases its appraisal system solely on those values we have been implicitly advocating will not necessarily produce the intended, desired and expected results. As will be shown in later chapters, apart from promoting goodwill towards organisational members, the appraisal system must contain the hard characteristics of clear targets, sound data and purposeful review.

VARIETIES OF APPRAISAL

It is important to recognise that appraisal may have a number of different purposes, some of which are clearly geared to the needs of the organisation, some to the needs of the individuals within that organisation, and some to the needs of both. Our concept of appraisal, while unquestionably also concerned with self-development, includes also processes for assessing concurrently an individual's performance in discharging specific and agreed responsibilities and his developmental needs in order that he may either take on further responsibilities or be able in the future better to fulfil his present role. That aspect of appraisal is what often goes by the name of *performance appraisal*.

PERFORMANCE APPRAISAL AND MERIT RATING

Performance appraisal may be confused, in ignorance or as a matter of policy, with merit rating, a technique appropriate only to judging the quantifiable outputs of operatives and craftsmen. Appraisal, properly used, will provide the organisation with far greater benefits than a mechanical procedure for judging managerial and professional merit payments. Indeed many expert writers on appraisal categorically state that the appraisal system should not be used for this purpose:

> Organisations attempting to develop their staff appraisal and develop-
> ment procedures are strongly advised to plan to keep the three activities
> of 'performance', 'reward' and 'potential' review not only separate in time
> but also in paperwork, procedure and responsibility.
>
> (Randall *et al.*, 1984)

There is no doubt that the political repercussions of any attempt to impose upon schools a link between performance appraisal and merit pay would be considerable. The Secretary of State for Education and Science is on record as confirming that such a link will not come about as a direct result of government policy. Nevertheless, there remains a danger that governing bodies, faced with making invidious decisions about the awarding of merit pay, may attempt, for want of any identifiable alternative, to use performance appraisal as a determinant.

THE POTENTIALITIES OF APPRAISAL

It is widely claimed that a well-run appraisal system:

- integrates the individual and the organisation;
- provides the opportunity to initiate problem-solving and counselling interviews;
- encourages self-development;
- provides the basis for an institutional audit;
- provides for the dissemination of career development advice;
- gives managers greater control through the setting of objectives;
- gives individuals greater clarity of purpose through the provision of clear objectives, while allowing autonomy of method;
- helps to build collective morale;
- encourages and inspires individuals and enhances their self-esteem and self-confidence;
- reduces alienation, removes resentment, provides the opportunity for

subordinates to let off steam;
- allows for better vertical communication and the creation of a more open style of management;
- facilitates the identification of potential talent;
- enhances the communication of organisational aims to all staff and facilitates the coordination of effort;
- channels individual effort into organisational goals;
- provides a mechanism whereby individual effort can be recognised even if no financial reward can be offered;
- provides a mechanism whereby the individual can influence the organisation.

No one system can achieve all the potential benefits of appraisal, both because the climates and circumstances of organisations differ, and because some of the potential benefits may, in any given organisation, prove to be incompatible. In one organisation the climate may favour individual support and encouragement; in another, high achievement and goal orientation. One organisation may need to emphasise individualism, entrepreneurial activities and self-development, another to focus more narrowly on achieving specific objectives within tight resource constraints. Again, the nature of appraisal as viewed by one organisation may be developmental: to review and plan what action will best contribute to the development of individual members of staff. Another may see appraisal as more concerned with maximising performance: to inform and develop each member so as to extract the maximum benefit for the service. Any single system which tried to combine all the possible benefits of appraisal would probably create such a confused multi-targeted approach, with conflicting objectives and resource demands, that it would fail. Consequently, the designers of a system must be clear about which of the possible benefits they are seeking and construct their system to achieve those objectives, even at the cost of ignoring other, no less valuable potential outcomes.

MODELS OF STAFF APPRAISAL

Figure 1.1 shows four 'ideal' types of appraisal interview. The horizontal axis denotes whether the emphasis is on individual or organisational goals: that is, whether the main concern is for the growth of the individual as a means to organisational development or whether the interests of the organisation are paramount. The vertical axis indicates the extent to which management sees itself as having a proactive role: that is, whether its concern is the setting of objectives or performance targets, the identification of training needs, reaching agreement on suitable developmental tasks, taking or sharing responsibility for developmental growth and the achievement of objectives. The salient features of the four basic types are listed in Figure 1.2.

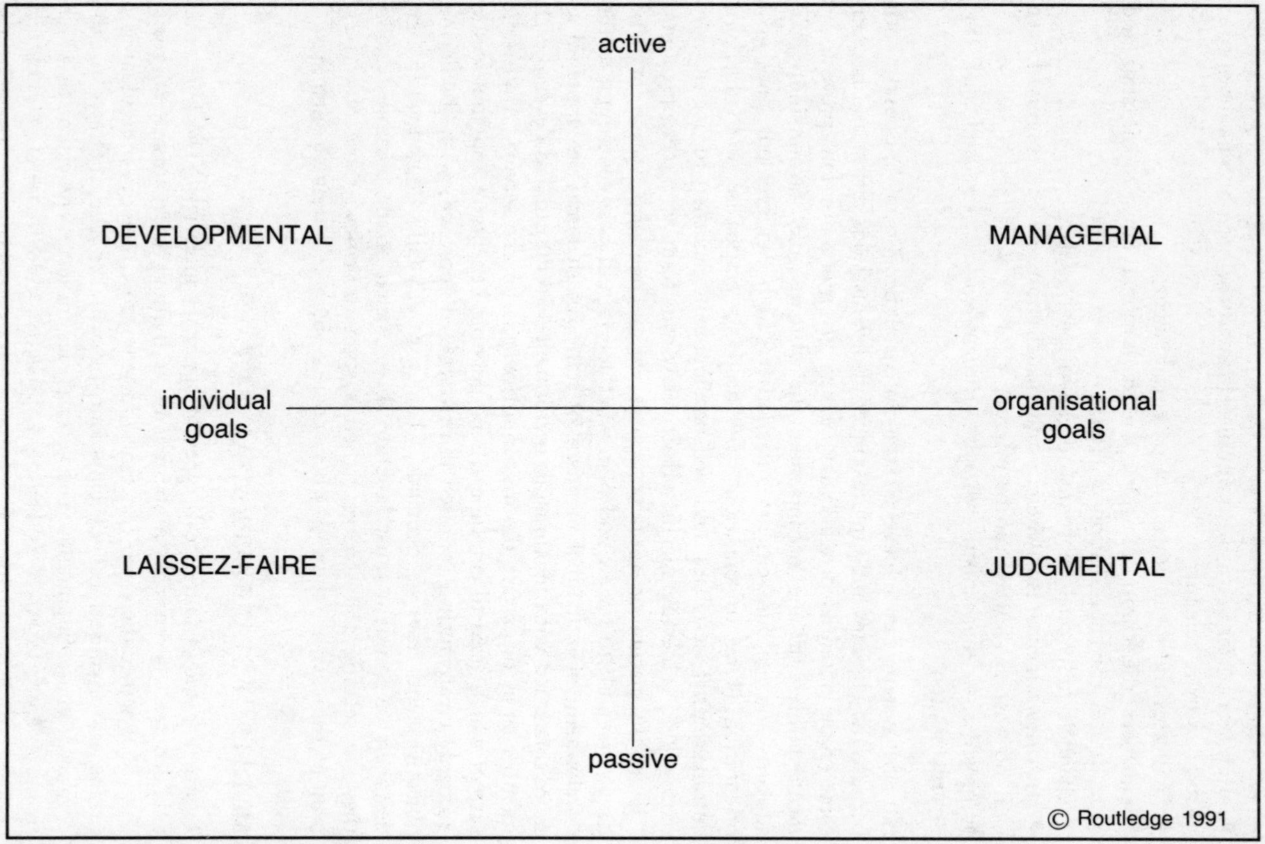

active   passive

organisational goals

individual goals

DEVELOPMENTAL

MANAGERIAL

LAISSEZ-FAIRE

JUDGMENTAL

© Routledge 1991

Figure 1.1 Types of appraisal interview

Figure 1.2 Key features of the four basic types

DEVELOPMENTAL	MANAGERIAL
Assumes professional, collegial and collective authority to lie within the profession	Assumes right to manage: hierarchical position confirms authority.
Concerned with truth, accuracy and the maintenance of moral, ethical and professional values	Concerned with doing and achieving, efficiency and effectiveness
Appraisals of colleagues are made by peers, based on public information	Appraisals of subordinates are made by superordinates
Assumes self-motivation towards personal and professional development	Sets objectives and targets to maximise achievement of organisational objectives
Bipartite approach towards enabling self-improvement	Uses incentives and praise
Designed to produce agreed programme with a shared responsibility to achieve objectives	Motivates subordinate by setting short-term goals and by periodic review
Concerned with longer-term professional development	Concerned with shorter-term assessment of performance
Marked by trust, openness and cooperation	
LAISSEZ-FAIRE	**JUDGMENTAL**
Recognises the importance of self-development	Uses system to maintain social control
Management abdicates from responsibility	Manager assumes that his position authorises him to make judgments
Subordinate permitted to raise and discuss issues	Manager collects data for assessment of subordinate
Lack of focus, direction and purpose in system	Individuals are rated one against another
Believes in importance of self-motivation	Assumes extrinsic motivation necessary
Follow-up left to subordinate	System used for merit rating and performance-related payments

© Routledge 1991

The movement in the 1970s towards humanistic psychology had a considerable influence on our concepts of management. Today the trend is increasingly towards a recognition of the value of individuals within the organisation and of their autonomy and self-actualising potential. The days when organisations could map out the career progression of the new recruit from entry to retirement have passed. Nowadays individuals are more and more seen to be responsible for managing their own careers, for determining their preferred goals, for assessing their own capabilities and their developmental needs. Yet, despite this healthy recognition of individual potential, it remains a truism that few people are wholly able to judge their own capacities, strengths and weaknesses without the catalyst of some form of appraisal, whether by peer or line manager.

There are clearly strengths and weaknesses in each of the four systems. The left-hand polarity of the horizontal axis emphasises individual responsibility but may place excessive reliance on the ability of individuals to make sound judgments and to recognise those occasions when the needs of the organisation may override those of the person. The right-hand polarity may be effective in setting institutional goals and making objective judgments but may fail to capitalise on the internal strengths of individuals.

The emphasis on objectives and yardsticks characteristic of the managerial type of appraisal has been criticised on several grounds: that the rapidity of change may well invalidate or modify the goals that the managers have set; that lower echelon staff may have little control over the factors that affect goal achievement; and, particularly true of education, despite the present emphasis on the identification of performance criteria, that there are large areas in which specific targets cannot be identified and which may be undervalued in any review of activity. At the same time it must be recognised that the autonomy of the school is being diminished by the National Curriculum and by financial systems. These, while ostensibly designed to promote freedom and flexibility, nevertheless have their own inbuilt constraints and rigidities. One consequence is that the managerial approach may well increasingly commend itself to those to whom the school is deemed accountable.

Where any school places itself on these two axes – or is placed by the combined or conflicting influences of central government, local education authority and governing body – will be a powerful determinant of the type of appraisal system which it will adopt.

Chapter 2

The evolution of appraisal

The main concern of this chapter is to chart the path by which appraisal has come about in England and Wales in order to inform and illuminate the training considerations which follow. The widely accepted starting point is 'The Great Debate', initiated by James Callaghan in 1976 and calling for higher standards and greater accountability in education. Seminal though that speech was, some years were to pass before the first official document signalled the likelihood of a specific national programme of teacher appraisal. There could have been no more unfortunate introduction to such a significant innovation than the statement which appeared in *Teaching Quality* (DES, 1983):

> Concern for quality demands that [where] teachers fail to maintain a satisfactory standard of performance, employers must . . . be ready to use procedures for dismissal.

Not surprisingly this statement roused the ire of the teaching profession and the resultant hubbub drowned out the many excellent features of that publication. At a time when the fall in pupil numbers was beginning to lead to expectations of better conditions and resources, teachers, rightly or wrongly, saw appraisal as the means by which the teaching force would be drastically reduced. 'What percentage of teachers', asked the cynics, 'would be judged as having failed "to maintain a satisfactory standard of performance"? Why, that percentage which would obviate the extra expenditure needed to reduce class size.' For teachers and LEAs alike, the first priority at a time of considerable turbulence in the educational atmosphere was the in-service training of staff to improve their competence. LEA officers maintained that they already had at their disposal the machinery for ceasing to employ unsatisfactory teachers. Advisers were skilled in indicating to no-hopers that they were in the wrong profession and in helping them to exit gracefully; and, if necessary, dismissal procedures could be invoked for those who were unwilling to heed advice. It is true that these procedures were, and still are, lengthy but that is because they are circumscribed by conditions and rights of appeal that ensure that no teacher is wrongfully dismissed.

The statement by the then Secretary of State, Sir Keith Joseph, in his speech to the North of England Education Conference in January 1984 may have been intended as a palliative but did little to mollify teacher outrage:

> I attach particular importance to the interesting and innovative work . . . in the important area of teacher assessment and in the schemes of collective self-assessment within the schools.

It will be observed that he uses the term 'assessment'. There was in the early days a disturbing confusion between assessment, which is both judgmental and summative, and appraisal, which is developmental and formative. Sir Keith's reference to 'collective self-assessment', was, despite its inclusion of two hurrah words − 'collective' and 'self' − too vague to be helpful. One assumes that he was referring to the School Curriculum Development Committee project on whole school evaluation, the *Guidelines for Review and Internal Development in Schools* (GRIDS), which was then nearing completion after national trialling (McMahon *et al.*, 1984).

This confusion over terminology was to continue for some time and to bedevil relationships between the DES and teachers' unions. It was not a mere matter of semantics: underlying the choice of words undoubtedly were major differences of opinion over the fundamental purposes of appraisal. Many of those who were supportive of a strategy for school improvement and personal and professional development became chary of using the word appraisal lest its misuse nullified their good intentions. At a time when confusion and argument were at a peak, the DES belatedly but wisely commissioned from Suffolk LEA, one of the few with firsthand experience of the introduction of appraisal, a report which was later to be published under the title of *Those Having Torches* (Suffolk LEA, 1985). While there were many who criticised the report's excessive reliance on research on appraisal in the USA, it nevertheless contains much that is valuable and thought-provoking. Above all, it contains two categorical statements that set the agenda for much of the discussion that was to follow. The first was in the form of what is being increasingly described as a 'mission statement':

> The corner-stone of appraisal schemes is the belief that teachers wish to improve their performance in order to enhance the education of pupils.

The second might well be called a shot across the bows of those who had commissioned the report:

> A precise definition of the purpose of the appraisal system is imperative: failure to do this can not only be inhibitory but is also downright disastrous.

The fact that an appreciable number of schools were already engaging in staff appraisal − whether or not they were calling it that is irrelevant − is often overlooked. Bunnell and Stephens (1984) described a voluntary scheme that had been introduced gradually and with the full cooperation of the staff of their Hertfordshire school. Their stance had been: 'If we want an appraisal scheme to match our needs and principles we must involve ourselves in the making of it'. This was the approach of a number of schools, some of which documented the development of their schemes, though few, if any, with the thoroughness and objectivity of Bunnell and Stephens. Turner and Clift (1985) published as the first stage of an Open University research project begun in October 1984 a register and review of schemes developed in over fifty schools. Newman (1985) conducted a survey 'to establish the pattern and practice of staff appraisal in secondary schools in the south and south-west of England'. Of 206 schools in the seven LEAs – a response rate of over 88 per cent – nearly one in four was in November 1984 already operating a staff appraisal scheme and a further seventeen schools were in the process of starting a scheme in the year of his enquiry. There is no means of knowing whether this pattern was replicated on the same scale in other geographical regions, but there is ample evidence that staff appraisal schemes were mushrooming, mainly as a strategy for school improvement. Indeed, so widespread was the interest in schemes that Newman found it necessary to warn that:

> While there are many common features in appraisal schemes operating in different schools, there is no single universal arrangement that will work for all. Experience shows that there may be difficulties if a school 'borrows' a scheme from another school and tries to use it without any attempt to see whether it is suitable or not.

That warning needs to be heeded even as we approach a national scheme. If it does not have within it sufficient flexibility to meet the needs of different management styles and structures, different approaches to learning, different staff experiences, then it may well become a strait-jacket rather than a strategy for improvement.

In the same year HMI produced a report *Quality in Schools: Evaluation and Appraisal* (HMI, 1985b) which was a consequence of a two-year survey of a number of LEAs and schools in which staff appraisal was taking place. In the report HMI attempted just such a definition as the Suffolk team had called for:

> Staff appraisal involves qualitative judgments about performance and, although it may start as self-appraisal by the teacher, it will normally involve judgments by other persons responsible for that teacher's work – a head of department or year, the headteacher, a member of the senior management team or an officer of the LEA. This appraisal may well (and usually does) include the identification of professional development needs.

The statement, well intentioned though it may have been, is flawed in two respects: it confuses appraisal with assessment, invoking 'judgments by other persons'; and, oddly, the language in which it is cast clearly has secondary school management structures in mind, even though primary schools outnumber secondary by over six to one.

LEGISLATION

> The Secretary of State may by regulations make provision for requiring LEAs or such other persons as may be prescribed, to secure that the performance of teachers to whom the regulations apply . . . is regularly appraised in accordance with such requirements as may be prescribed.
>
> (DES: Education (No. 2) Act of 1986)

Like so much else in this piece of legislation, enactment is through regulations hereinafter to be made and, perhaps more alarming, subject to reformulation without presentation to Parliament. Undoubtedly the then Secretary of State, Kenneth Baker, would have argued that it was not for him to prescribe the requirements, but for the LEAs selected for the pilot scheme to advise him through the National Steering Group (NSG).

Unfortunately, this 'seemingly innocuous' section of the Act, as Sallis (1988) describes it, has too many loopholes for comfort: 'such other persons as may be prescribed' opens up the possibility of agencies other than LEAs being made responsible for appraisal procedures; 'to whom the regulations apply' is a phrase that leaves one wondering to which teachers they may not apply; and the open-endedness of 'such requirements as may be prescribed' has made many teachers and administrators fearful that all the efforts of the pilot schemes and the many valuable training experiences of other LEAs may be nullified by *diktat*.

The pilot study began in January 1987, immediately following the report of the ACAS Appraisal/Training Working Group (ACAS, 1986). The DES had selected six LEAs representing a geographic and demographic cross-section, a wide range of experience of appraisal and, so it seemed, an even wider range of expectations of the outcomes of a national appraisal scheme. Those six LEAs were Croydon, Cumbria, Newcastle, Salford, Somerset and Suffolk. The National Development Centre for School Management Training (NDC) was appointed as national coordinator and the Cambridge Institute of Education (CIE) as national evaluator.

Some of the misgivings to which the Act had given rise were dissipated by the open behaviour of the pilot authorities and particularly of the NDC. An interim report was presented to a national conference in May 1988 and published by the NDC immediately following the conference. The final report, *School Teacher Appraisal: A National Framework* (HMSO, 1989) sets out the findings of nearly two years of intensive work.

A NATIONAL FRAMEWORK

The NSG report was circulated in October 1989 to all Chief Education Officers, along with a survey (DES, 1989b) by HMI of developments in appraisal in the six pilot schemes and in other LEAs. In a covering letter the DES indicated that the new Secretary of State, John MacGregor, was proposing a six-month consultation period, an approach that contrasted markedly with the hustle of his predecessor, whose consultation norm was six weeks. Furthermore, he had decided that:

> in view of the far reaching reforms on which schools are now engaged it would not be right to make Regulations in the near future which required *all* schools to introduce appraisal within the next few years.
>
> (DES 1989a)

It will at first sight appear strange, not to say perverse, that the reaction of many educationists was one of disappointment. After all, were they not complaining constantly of 'innovation fatigue': GCSE, LFM, LMS among others? Yet their disappointment was explicable for several very cogent reasons. First, this was one innovation – possibly the only one in the decade – in the planning of which teachers' representatives at national and local level had been scrupulously involved. Secondly, appraisal had skilfully been steered away from a judgmental process to a developmental process, and was now one that many teachers saw as helpful to their professional development and the improvement of pupil learning. Thirdly, increasingly during the previous two years teachers and administrators in an appreciable number of LEAs had begun to grapple with the evolution of a strategy for the introduction of appraisal, had seen the appointment, under various titles, of LEA coordinators for appraisal and had set up their own pilot training schemes in collaboration with consultancies and higher education establishments. Finally, there was a growing realisation that appraisal could well be the key to the successful management of these other innovations.

If the Secretary of State had professed himself committed to allowing a greater lead-in time for a national scheme of appraisal, then there would have been little anxiety in the profession. As so often before, LEAs were faced with instituting a massive training programme in a short time and with many doubts as to where the skilled trainers would come from. Yet the same letter that announced the revised intentions also, most unusually, gave *carte blanche* to LEAs to veer training money available under the LEA Training Grants Scheme for the financial year 1990–91 from appraisal to 'other national priority training'. Inevitably, this gave rise to suspicions that he might be backtracking on appraisal entirely or considering a cheaper, less effective system.

The early reaction of the teacher unions was predictable and understandable. The NASUWT refused to cooperate with any appraisal scheme unless the Secretary of State for Education gave an assurance that he was prepared to accept the NSG's guidelines. Their spokesperson pointed out that 'the purpose of the pilots had been to devise a national scheme. Now that this had been put on the back-burner, there would be little point in cooperating with the pilot schemes' (TES, 1989b). The NUT stated that teachers could only be required to participate in appraisal within an agreed national framework. AMMA was prepared to accept schemes in the six pilot authorities provided that participation was voluntary and in line with the NSG recommendations and additionally, other schemes that met these criteria. It is clear that the action of the Secretary of State in, ostensibly, relieving schools of a major pressure had in fact provoked much teacher opposition at a time when he was doubtless trying to represent himself to them as having a greater concern for their professional well-being than his predecessor.

It is more likely that the problem of adequately resourcing this innovation lay at the heart of this change of attitude: £40 million a year had been quoted as the cost of appraisal. There is also the possibility that, consequently, this Secretary of State, like his predecessor, was attracted to practices in the USA: simpler, superficially less costly, but far less effective in securing school improvement and personal and professional development as we demonstrate in the next chapter. John Heywood, a prominent member of the Secondary Heads Association and a member of the NSG expressed the widespread concern felt nationally at this time:

> It would help if Mr MacGregor . . . recognised that he already has within his grasp the 'nationally agreed framework'. To impose an alternative scheme would undoubtedly fail to secure support from the teaching profession as a whole.
>
> (Heywood, 1989)

Whether or not these views were to influence the Secretary of State is unlikely ever to be known. However, in January 1990, he denied with some vehemence that he had 'gone cold on appraisal':

> It remains our aim that practical, effective schemes of appraisal should be implemented in all LEAs just as soon as practicable. But I agree entirely with the view of the National Steering Group on Appraisal that its introduction needs to be managed very carefully and sensitively . . . . Consultation will last until Easter [1990]. Thereafter I propose to issue guidance to schools and LEAs. I envisage that this guidance will be followed, as soon as practicable, by regulations requiring the introduction of schemes of appraisal across England and Wales within a fixed period.
>
> (MacGregor, 1990a)

In the event, he decided not to issue regulations at all. He chose the occasion of the British Education Management and Administration Society (BEMAS) conference in September 1990 to announce that he had decided against making appraisal obligatory. He adduced two reasons: the first, that schools were already heavily burdened with other major innovations, in particular with 'massive efforts involved in introducing the National Curriculum'; the second that: 'Appraisal is essentially a management issue. Our general policy is that decisions about the way schools and teachers are managed should be taken locally' (MacGregor, 1990c).

The decision on whether or not to introduce appraisal is to rest with teachers' employers, the LEA except for voluntary aided and grant maintained schools. Once the employer so decides, appraisal will obtain for all teachers in that LEA or school. He gives no period of time by which this will have to be achieved.

It is inconceivable that this radical change in government policy was not influenced, even dictated, by the Treasury's view of the cost implications. The Secretary of State has now authorised a mere £9 million a year for three years beginning 1991–2 for *both training and implementation*. Thereafter funding specifically for appraisal will cease.

The Secretary of State's argument runs thus:

> In most other walks of life appraisal schemes, once bedded in, are not specifically funded at all – they are a normal part of good personnel management. The time which they require is more than repaid through the greater effectiveness of the staff appraised.

> (MacGregor, 1990c)

This is flawed logic. In other walks of life – the Civil Service, industrial management, banking, for example – it is relatively easy for arrangements to be made so that both appraiser and appraisee are freed for the appraisal interview with no significant interference on the smooth running of the concern. Appraisal can, indeed, be bedded in. For the school there is no way in which the clients – the pupils – are unaffected, since if their class teacher is either appraising or being appraised they are not being taught unless cover is provided. That cover has to be paid for from the school's budget; it will always be an on-cost, which, unless met from DES funding, will inevitably have a deleterious effect on the availability of facilities for learning.

The time costs of appraisal

Although the NSG interim report (NDC, 1988) recommended appraisal annually for teachers and biennially or triennially for headteachers, the final report recommended (para 8) that for both it be conducted on a two-year cycle. Furthermore, the NSG final report recommended that the number of appraisees per appraiser be limited to four over the two-year cycle (para 16). The reduction from five to four was a recognition of the considerable time costs of appraisal, particularly in the introductory phase, and of the pressure that this would impose on managers already heavily committed.

Both recommendations were supported implicitly by the HMI report which in a section on costing (para 93) estimated that 'the operation of a [biennial] national appraisal system in schools which allows for release for the process itself and some ongoing training will require the equivalent of 1,800 additional teachers'. Elsewhere the HMI report (DES, 1989b, para 8) points out that the 'current shortages of teachers in some parts of the country and in some subjects suggest that the additional staffing may not be readily available'. The fact that there are acute regional variations in teacher availability undoubtedly influenced the DES to leave to LEAs the decision of whether or not to embark upon appraisal.

Secondary schools will be hard pressed to 'bed in' appraisal. Many have already invested a great deal of time and energy in planning for appraisal, often bearing all but the training costs from their own limited resources. Yet headteachers of small primary schools in full charge of a class will find it impossible if this time cost is not somehow met. They have no way of releasing themselves or their teachers for classroom observation or the appraisal interview.

The purpose of appraisal

The NSG report reiterates the view of the ACAS report that appraisal should be understood

> not as a series of perfunctory periodic events, but as a continuous and systematic process intended to help individual teachers with their professional development and career planning, and to help ensure that the in-service training and deployment of teachers matches the complementary needs of individual teachers and the schools.
>
> (ACAS, 1986)

The NSG report goes further (para 11) in urging that 'appraisal should be used positively to promote equal opportunities by encouraging all teachers to fulfil their potential as teachers'. The merit of these statements is that there is a clear rejection of appraisal as a device for managerial control, and an emphasis on appraisal as a strategy for professional development. Within this context the phrase 'deployment of teachers' appears to have none of the threatening undercurrents, feared by teachers in the days when appraisal was first being mooted, that it might be used to justify cost-cutting exercises regardless of teachers' proficiency. Nevertheless, the teaching profession will have to be on the watch lest market force philosophies lead to abuse of this declaration.

The appraisal process

The draft National Framework (DES, 1990b) comes down firmly for appraisal by line managers. It is reasonable that the decision on who is to appraise whom rests with the headteacher, though that does not rule out the making of that decision through consultation and negotiation; a free-for-all system of choice would give rise to considerable managerial complexity. Nevertheless, there should be room for schools which have less hierarchical management structures to plan their appraisal schemes to suit their own conditions. One school with which we have worked for some time has set up a structure based upon interdisciplinary groupings of staff in which different levels of management are represented. This approach is an adaptation of the quality circles system, common in Japanese industry but by no means confined to that country or culture. In it the representative of senior management acts as facilitator and 'problems [connected with their own sphere of work] are identified by the individuals rather than by senior management [and] identified problems and solutions are presented to management for decisions and implementation' (Wallace, 1986; see also Robson, 1984). It would be a sad departure from our long tradition of local autonomy if this school and others like it were debarred from locking their appraisal systems into existing management systems merely because they did not conform to the norm.

We are led to the conclusion that the decision to have biennial appraisal has been made, not on educational criteria, but because of the cost. The natural appraisal cycle for the majority of teachers – those broadly described as classroom teachers rather than managers – is the academic year. It is for this period that, in our experience, the majority of goals are set. The HMI report included firm evidence that this view is supported by those institutions which contributed to their enquiry (para 38):

> Of 218 institutions responding to the question of how often they intended that staff should be appraised, 60 per cent said annually, 9 per cent answered every two years and the others had no view about what would be desirable or possible.

> (DES, 1989b)

It is also the view strongly maintained by the teachers' unions and most cogently expressed by the NUT (1981, 1985).

It may well be that schools which have experienced the benefits of annual appraisal will be reluctant to see what they would regard as a watered-down version. Indeed, it is arguable that the greater the rate of change in our educational institutions, the greater the need to correlate teacher performance and developmental needs against the changing scenario of whole school policy.

The components of teacher appraisal are set out in the draft National

Framework (paras 12–21) and in greater detail in the NSG report: the initial meeting (para 30); self-appraisal (para 32); classroom observation (paras 33–36); data collection (paras 37–39 and 45); the appraisal interview itself (paras 40–43); the preparation of the appraisal statement (para 44); and follow up/formal review (para 45). The detailed recommendations of most of these paragraphs are subsumed in those chapters of this book which deal specifically with appraisal training for each of these purposes.

One element, however, deserves comment in this chapter rather than later: data collection. Rightly, the NSG report (para 37) points out that 'there are other sources of information about a teacher's teaching [in addition to classroom observation] . . . including the work and progress of pupils'. Put thus, the statement is unexceptionable. However, many teachers are seriously concerned that the key stage attainment tests of the National Curriculum may be used as the most readily available 'objective' evidence of pupils' progress. This they may be. They are not, however, valid measures of teacher performance. Pupil progress depends on a host of factors over which the classroom teacher has no control: home circum-stances, previous learning experiences, physical resources, LEA support and so on. The publication of SATs by schools is already regarded as a divisive practice, too easily misinterpreted by those who do not know the precise circumstances of the school. The inclusion of this information in the data for teacher appraisal brings that same divisiveness down to the personal level, running counter to the corporate concern for school standards of performance that all staff ought to have and maintain.

The report continues (para 38) by referring to the need to 'take account of all aspects of a teacher's job [including] pastoral duties and administrative responsibilities' and points out that this 'may involve consulting other teachers in the school'. The DES has wisely drawn up a Code of Practice which we believe to be so important that we have included it verbatim as Appendix 1 to this book.

The NSG report makes a distinction between appraisal for assistant teachers and for headteachers which we believe to be untenable: 'If appraisal is to be meaningful it must be conducted against the background of certain expectations about teachers and teaching, and in the case of headteachers, the management and leadership of schools' (para 62). The implication that management and leadership is restricted to the function of headship takes no account of the realities of school management today. It may be considered too glib to urge that all teachers today are managers; but undeniably the management role is exercised, in part by delegation, in part by involvement in corporate decision making, by increasing numbers of teachers in our schools. The introduction of the post of curriculum coordinator in the primary school has entrusted many main professional grade teachers with important managerial responsibilities that go far beyond the exercise of a mere administrative function. Increasingly, as the demands of the National Curriculum have had to be disseminated to staff, the curriculum coordinator has had to undertake key responsibilities for training, monitoring, evaluating and stabilising. The weight of national innovation in this and other fields has led primary headteachers to consider, if they had not already done so, the merits of more collegiate forms of school management; and the job specifications of deputy heads and postholders increasingly reflect this.

For secondary schools it has long been apparent that the appraisal of middle and senior managers must reflect these managerial responsibilities. Indeed, while teaching performance is a basic concern of appraisal, it must be recognised that there are some members of staff – not only the headteacher – for whom the exploration of other performance criteria is far more vital to the health of the institution. We feel that this is of sufficient importance to merit a chapter devoted to the ways in which management performance can be appraised.

Chapter 3

Appraisal USA

Teacher appraisal, more usually called teacher evaluation for reasons which will become apparent, has been increasingly introduced in the United States since the mid-1970s. That experience and the wealth of research into the effectiveness of evaluation procedures can be of considerable value to us, but only if we recognise from the outset both the similarities and the differences in the educational history, climate and culture of the two countries.

During the 1960s and 1970s both the UK and the USA went through a stage of unprecedented public expenditure on education. In the UK we were still at that time more preoccupied with the provision of physical resources, both to compensate for the effects of wartime destruction of schools and to provide for the replacement of a selective system of secondary education by comprehensive schooling for all, and therefore we were less affected by what Hord (1987) describes as a 'bewildering array of new demands and possibilities [that] brought with it staggering logistic difficulties'. Less affected is, however, only a matter of degree. Those of us who managed schools in that period look back on it as a time of high innovation and rapid, often inchoate change.

It was not long before there arose on both sides of the Atlantic cries for accountability, initially in the form of 'Are we getting value for money in these high-cost innovative curriculum developments?' While this is a reasonable question to ask of any enterprise, there was little recognition that innovation is a lengthy process as it goes through the stages of planning, preparation, trialling, refinement, dissemination, evaluation and, finally, stabilisation. Evaluation became the catchword, even though the process had in many cases scarcely begun.

At first it was clear – or seemed to be at the time – that it was the innovation which was being evaluated and the innovators who were being held accountable. Gradually, almost imperceptibly, the focus appeared to shift. Initially attention had been concentrated on development: of content, of class organisation, of teaching style. Soon it was to switch to outcomes. During the 1970s it became evident that 'the demand for accountability in education [had] shifted from broad issues of finance and program management to specific concerns about the quality of classroom teaching and teachers' (Darling-Hammond *et al.*, 1983). Later, though not much later, this same demand was to be articulated in the UK.

EVALUATION LEGISLATION

Although there had been compulsory evaluation of teacher performance in the USA since the mid-1970s in a number of states – Oklahoma, for example, has had teacher evaluation requirements since 1977 – there has recently been a considerable upsurge of attention to the process. As is doubtless well known, there can be no federal legislation in matters of this kind: the states themselves enact what they individually deem to be required. Thus:

> The Oklahoma Legislature mandated major revisions in the law in 1985. The intent of the revisions is to improve the quality of teaching and administrative performance. The 1985 law required that minimum criteria for evaluation be developed by the State Board of Education for teaching and administrative appraisal. A committee of educators *and parents* was appointed . . . to write the minimum criteria. Based on research in effective schools and teaching strategies, the criteria were approved and adopted.
>
> (Oklahoma, 1989)

Texas, on the other hand, appears to have had no statewide appraisal system before 1986, though it is evident that teacher evaluation systems were in place in most of the school districts within the state. In 1984:

> [The state legislature] directed the State Board of Education to adopt an appraisal process and criteria with which to appraise the performance of teachers *for career ladder purposes*. The Legislature mandated that the criteria be based upon observable job-related behaviors. The State Board of Education was further directed to provide:
>
> (1) at least two appraisals during each of the two appraisal periods within the regular school year;
> (2) a uniform training program for appraisers of teacher performance, including uniform appraiser certification standards; and
> (3) *inclusion of teacher self-appraisal in the appraisal process.*
>
> (Texas, 1988)

(Note: in 1987 the first requirement was modified to an annual appraisal for all teachers beyond a certain level of experience and standard. The time costs were clearly too heavy.)

The italics are ours throughout the above citations. It is interesting to note that in Oklahoma parents were involved in the development of performance criteria, a practice that would not find favour with many teachers in the UK. This was not the case in Texas. There the Texas Education Agency:

[having] conducted a review of literature on teaching effectiveness, surveyed other states where statewide appraisal systems had been implemented, and gathered information from 156 school districts in Texas regarding the teacher evaluation systems used in those districts . . . [produced] a job-relatedness survey which had as items those behaviors identified in the previous processes [and invited 30,000 teachers to respond to them in terms of] observability, importance and frequency of use.

(Texas, 1988)

The implication of 'career ladder purposes' are both positive and negative. The Texas Administrative Code for appraisal specifies that 'the result of the appraisal of teachers shall be used for career ladder' – that is, incremental and promotional – 'and staff development purposes' and 'may be used for contract renewal purposes'. The Texas Teacher Appraisal System is recorded in over 200 pages of *Teacher Orientation Manual* and *Appraiser's Manual*. Through scrupulously documented performance indicators, scored numerically and translated centrally into standards ranging from 'unsatisfactory' to 'clearly outstanding', the system seeks to assess teacher performance. It accepts that 'although classroom teaching is the primary focus of the performance appraisal, no single model of teaching is mandated by the statewide teacher appraisal system'. It includes a well structured two-part self-appraisal document for 'instructional goals and outcomes' which teachers share with their supervisors and which include the opportunity to 'identify way(s) in which the district, your supervisor, and/or staff development activities can assist you in this endeavor'.

A more pessimistic approach to appraisal in the USA is exemplified in the use of the Oklahoma criteria (see pages 27–8 below) by Milburn District in that state. 'The rating scale', the district proforma states, 'assumes that every practitioner can improve or change'. We doubt if anyone would disagree with this assumption. It continues, however, by laying down a four-point classification of the subsequent performance indicators which would surely cast a mantle of gloom and despondency over most of the teachers in this district:

A: appropriate level of performance
G: room for growth
N: needs an immediate plan for improvement
U: unsatisfactory.

(Oklahoma, 1989)

Any classification of this kind, if it is to be effective, must be clearly unambiguous and hierarchical. We, were we appraising through such a system, would be much exercised to differentiate between the first two classifications. Do we not all have room for growth? And, given that we do, is our level of performance necessarily less than appropriate?

Not surprisingly, the highly negative focus of this evaluation report leads for some teachers to a 'plan for improvement' in which 'the evaluator and the professional will identify objectives for improvement by referring to the criteria for evaluation . . . The teacher is warned that failure to improve according to the plan may result in a recommendation for termination of employment'.

APPRAISAL OBJECTIVES IN THE USA

'Termination of appointment' rings alarm bells in the minds of many teachers in the UK. One can almost hear them saying: 'If that is what appraisal might be about, we want nothing to do with it'. They may be relieved to know that, after the initial, non-tenured probationary period has been successfully completed, the termination of contract of a teacher in the USA is nearly as difficult to bring about as it is in this country. The term 'hire and fire' is used far too glibly, both within the US educational system and by us in the UK when we talk about it. Rightly, superintendents in the district and state departments of education demand that every possible step has been taken within the school and the system to help a teacher to overcome difficulties, and require too that these have been scrupulously documented, before termination of employment is even considered. Furthermore, teacher unions are no less protective of their members' interests on that side of the Atlantic than on this.

The purposes of the appraisal system in the USA can be summed up as follows:

- to define the skills that teachers should demonstrate in classrooms;
- to develop the abilities of teachers and appraisers alike to recognise these skills in action;
- to use the system to evaluate teacher performance;
- to use the system as a mechanism to upgrade or improve skills.

While evaluation of performance is still a consideration in teacher appraisal in the USA, there is much evidence that increasingly appraisal systems are focusing on the development by principals and other senior members of staff of a range of supportive skills: in identifying areas in need of attention; in working collegially with teachers in the constuction of growth plans; and in providing professional advice for enhancing performance. The main system goals are therefore concerned with improvement and not with termination.

There is still, it must be said, a preoccupation with performance ratings in the USA, possibly influenced by the much higher profile there for statistical research in education. The 'value for money' of the time spent in number-crunching is in some states being increasingly called into question. The overriding consideration is surely whether or not complex analyses of performance scores, such as those used in Texas, actually contribute to the improvement of interactions between teachers and their students. Of that there must be considerable doubt.

PERFORMANCE CRITERIA

Any misgivings we may have about differences between the educational systems and priorities of the two English-speaking nations should not blind us to the skill with which effective teaching – the transatlantic use of the alternative word 'instruction' suggests a higher degree of differentiation than necessarily exists in practice – has been analysed into performance criteria. It may well be that we are in danger in the UK of engaging in classroom observation with only a vague idea of what we are looking for. It has been comparatively rare even for advisers within an LEA to have uniform checklists, though, as the need for greater precision and commonalty have become evident, an increasing number of LEA teams have begun to structure their own. The ACAS Agreement (ACAS, 1986) includes at Annex E a teacher entry grade prompt list containing *inter alia* classroom observation performance criteria which would undoubtedly be useful at all levels in the profession; but that for main profesional grade teachers, Annex C, admittedly published with the proviso that 'this list . . . may need modification in the light of the experience gained during the Pilot Study', is perfunctory. In the absence as yet of national performance criteria and in the belief that teachers will be actively involved either at school level or on LEA consultative committees in the drawing up of criteria appropriate to classroom observation, we include on the following pages the performance criteria for the states of Oklahoma and New Mexico, believing that, at the very least, they will provide a starting point for consideration of criteria relevant to the UK educational climate and culture.

The Oklahoma State Department of Education handbook demonstrates its commitment to good learning practice by inviting its teachers, as a preliminary exercise, to match criteria with definitions. Trainers in the UK may well consider this a good introductory training exercise for any discussion of effective teaching criteria, noting its emphasis on positive behaviours. The example from New Mexico has fewer categories, but these are elaborated in greater detail. We have retained US spelling and usage.

Minimum criteria for effective teaching performance: Oklahoma

I   PRACTICE

A   Teacher Management Indicators

1   Preparation
The teacher plans for delivery of the lesson relative to short-term and long-term objectives.
2   Routine
The teacher uses minimum class time for non-instructional routines thus maximizing time on task.
3   Discipline
The teacher clearly defines expected behavior (encourages positive behavior and controls negative behavior).
4   Learning Environment
The teacher establishes rapport with students and provides a pleasant, safe and orderly climate conducive to learning.

B   Teacher Instructional Indicators

1   Establishes Objectives
The teacher communicates the instructional objectives to students.
2   Stresses Sequence
The teacher shows how the present topic is related to those topics that have been taught or that will be taught.
3   Relates Objectives
The teacher relates subject topics to existing student experiences.
4   Involves All Learners
The teacher uses signaled responses, questioning techniques and/or guided practices to involve all students.
5   Explains Content
The teacher teaches the objectives through a variety of methods.
6   Explains Directions
The teacher gives directions that are clearly stated and related to the learning objectives.

© Routledge 1991

7 Models
The teacher demonstrates the desired skills.
8 Monitors
The teacher checks to determine if students are progressing toward stated objectives.
9 Adjusts Based on Monitoring
The teacher changes instruction based on the results of monitoring.
10 Guides Practice
The teacher requires all students to practice newly learned skills while under the direct supervision of the teacher.
11 Provides for Independent Practice
The teacher requires students to practice newly learned skills without the direct supervision of the teacher.
12 Establishes Closure
The teacher summarizes and fits into context what has been taught.

II PRODUCTS

A Teacher Product Indicators

1 Lesson Plans
The teacher writes daily lesson plans designed to achieve the identified objectives.
2 Student Files
The teacher maintains a written record of student progress.
3 Grading Patterns
The teacher utilizes grading patterns that are fairly administered and based on identified criteria.

B Student Achievement Indicators

Students demonstrate mastery of the stated objectives through projects, daily assignments, performance and test scores.

Teaching competencies: Lovington District, New Mexico

I: The teacher communicates accurately and effectively in the content area and maintains a professional rapport with students by:

- communicating accurate and up-to-date knowledge;
- providing accurate oral and written communications;
- communicating to students the instructional intent of the plan at the start;
- communicating involvement and interest in the lesson;
- giving clear directions and explanations relating to the lesson;
- communicating clearly and concisely;
- demonstrating confidence in his/her abilities;
- modeling and encouraging constructive behavior patterns.

II: The teacher obtains feedback from and communicates with students in a manner which enhances student learning and understanding by:

- assuring that learners recognize the purpose and importance of the lesson;
- clarifying directions and explanations if students do not understand;
- giving reasonable explanations for actions, directions and decisions;
- encouraging appropriate student-to-student as well as student-to-teacher interactions;
- reinforcing and encouraging students' own efforts to be involved;
- communicating regularly with students about their needs and progress;
- providing constructive feedback to students about their behavior.

III: The teacher appropriately utilizes a variety of teaching methods and resources for each area taught:

- selecting content and a variety of materials for lessons;
- using teaching methods, materials and media which address student learning levels, rates and styles;

- providing opportunities and materials for students to apply or practice the knowledge or skills learned;
- implementing the learning activities in a logical sequence;
- working with individuals, small and large groups when appropriate;
- providing for students to work independently.

IV: The teacher encourages the development of student involvement, responsibility and critical thinking skills by:

- using techniques to arouse student interest;
- using appropriate questioning techniques;
- providing opportunities for the active involvement of students;
- allowing opportunities for student thought, speculation and creativity;
- using student responses and questions for teaching;
- giving students opportunities to make appropriate choices in and take responsibility for their own learning;
- providing reteaching, impromptu learning and other adjustments.

V: The teacher manages the classroom to ensure the best use of time by:

- handling routine tasks promptly and efficiently;
- minimizing distractions and interruptions;
- having materials or media ready for student use;
- handling individual behavior problems individually when possible.

VI: The teacher creates an atmosphere conducive to learning, self-discipline and the development of realistic and positive self-concepts by:

- establishing and stating expectations for behavior utilizing input from students;
- allowing opportunities for students to express personal ideas;
- being sensitive to needs and feelings of students;
- acknowledging students' achievements;
- assuring each student some success.

VII: The teacher displays evidence of planning instruction so that students achieve locally established objectives. The teacher indicates this by:

- specifying or selecting learner outcomes for each lesson;
- selecting procedures or strategies to achieve the expected outcomes;
- assuring outcomes are compatible with student abilities;
- maintaining planning documents and records.

VIII: The teacher gathers appropriate information about students and the results of instruction and uses that information to improve teaching performance. The teacher indicates this by:

- assessing student accomplishment on a regular basis;
- specifying or selecting materials and means to measure progress;
- assisting in the evaluation of the district in achieving expected outcomes;
- revising instruction when necessary to improve effectiveness;
- disseminating appropriate and understandable information.

IX: The teacher maintains a physical environment conducive to learning and appropriate to the maturity of the students. The teacher indicates this by:

- providing an attractive and orderly setting within resources;
- assuming responsibility for safety and health of students;
- adjusting the physical environment to accommodate a variety of styles and activities;
- organizing material appropriately and accessible to and for students.

X: The teacher presents a positive image of the school, district and profession and promotes understanding of educational needs and achievements. The teacher indicates this by:

- encouraging parent and community awareness of school progress and activities;
- maintaining appropriate confidentiality regarding students, parents and colleagues;
- discussing school, students and staff in a positive manner.

APPRAISAL IN PRACTICE IN THE USA

Through the good offices of Shirley Hord, a researcher and trainer whose work takes her regularly from state to state, we were able to have access to tapes of face-to-face or telephone interviews on appraisal conducted to an open interview schedule of our devising. The interviews covered a range of classroom teachers, principals and superintendents in four states. Our purpose was to discover the way in which appraisal was implemented and the regard in which it was held by practitioners at various levels.

In one state the superintendent made it clear that his only role as appraiser, other than for office personnel, was in relation to school principals. The documentation for principal appraisal had been devised largely by the principals themselves after broad areas of its content had been established with the superintendent. In this district appraisal had been introduced before state legislation and, although the state guidelines had been incorporated into the appraisal document, there appears to have been little need for radical alterations.

Completion of the appraisal form for principals takes place twice yearly. Additionally 'at the very end of the year each principal and I will sit down to work out growth plans for the school. Of course all that should be done all year round on a more informal basis and finally integrated into the formal evaluation instrument.' The curriculum coordinator plays a part in the evolution of the annual growth plan of the school and discussion with him or her may well form part of the data for the principal's appraisal.

The objective of the evaluation instrument, as far as the superintendent was concerned, was 'to evaluate how the principals deal with teachers, students, parents and immediate peers'. Asked whether or not this evaluation form did in fact achieve the objective, the superintendent showed a certain cynicism about all proformas: 'There's no such thing as a good instrument. If you find one, you send it to me please!' He had looked at instruments in other districts of his state: 'I have seen some extremely elaborate ones. There are those that are purely narrative, those that have complex checklists and those like ours which combine checklists with narrative. What matters most is that the principal feels comfortable with the instrument. If not, you will lose effectiveness. That's what I'm concerned about, not what instrument anyone comes up with.'

Relationships between superintendent and principals, and between principals and their staff, were his overriding consideration. 'If you are going to have an effective school, you need a close-knit group working together. Once you insert an evaluation of a colleague, I don't care what anyone says, any kind of instrument becomes a threat. Appraising is no fun, whichever way you cut it. It takes a real tightrope walker to make it work, a person who can make it clear that he wears a variety of hats: today my friend hat, tomorrow, when we talk about your growth plans, my monitoring and supporting hat, and next Wednesday, my evaluation hat. You need to keep those things very separate. It's hard to do and the real trick is to do it effectively.'

An elementary school principal, in another state, was far more preoccupied with the formalities of what she was expected to do.

Q. How often do you use this instrument with your teachers?

A. To keep me legal, for a non-tenured teacher I have to observe a lesson twice a year. I have to have a pre-conference with that teacher, tell her I am coming in the next day and let her know at what time. After the lesson I fill out this form and file it. At the Board meeting in March I present those evaluations and give my recommendation as to whether that teacher ought to be rehired or not. My recommendation goes before the Board together with the superintendent's report.

Q. What about any weaknesses you may have found during your lesson observations?

A. I have to have a post-conference as well as a pre-conference meeting with that teacher. If I have found an area where improvement is needed, I have to tell her what it is. If I find something that I feel needs immediate action, I have to set up a remediation plan.

Q. Do you then have an obligation to check back to see that the plan is being carried out effectively?

A. Yes. If I check off [tick that section of the form] that that teacher needs some immediate help, then I have to go back into that classroom after a little while. I give her time to get oriented, but I have to go back to see if she is correcting the faults I have observed.

Q. Is the report required to be signed by the teacher?

A. Yes, the teacher must sign the form.

Q. What if the teacher is in disagreement with your assessment? Does she have a right of appeal?

A. Whether she agrees or not, she must sign to say she has read it. In fact, I believe the wording on the form is 'I understand that my signature does not mean that I necessarily agree with this'.

Q. Is this form issued by the state department?

A. Yes. Before you can evaluate anyone, you have to go on an accreditation course of so many hours. The form I use contains all the minimum criteria that the state requires but we have added a few items that have local relevance.

In yet another state, the school principal of a small high school with a very high proportion of children of Hispanic parents was full of praise for the training he had received. 'Everyone has had an enormous amount of training in how to appraise. What's more, we have updating training every year.' Time is his problem, however; and he is led into a misconception of the nature and purpose of classroom observation which runs quite contrary to the appraisal principles established by his state board: 'With some teachers you can just walk in and you know who has got control, yet you are still supposed to spend at least 45 minutes in the classroom'.

Earlier he had spoken of the objectives of appraisal somewhat differently: 'to get a better documentation on the evaluation of teachers; to improve the teaching'. His objectives are markedly different from those of an assistant principal of a middle school in a neighbouring state.

Q. What do you see as the objectives of evaluation?

A. The main objectives are to select master teachers and to help teachers who are having problems. I have evaluated five teachers this year. Three I would consider to be master teachers, to the point that I recommended that they started providing information and guidance to other teachers.

Q. And for the teacher who is found lacking?

A. For an evaluation of such a teacher you don't go into the classroom just once, but three or four times, because you may not see in one visit everything you would like to see. If then you don't see effective teaching going on, if you are seeing uncorrected teacher behaviour, then you start on a different process entirely. That would probably be for termination.

Q. But before you reach that stage, is there not an intermediate step? Is there not a development or growth plan or suchlike?

A. Yes indeed. Since 1989 every teacher must develop with senior staff a growth plan in order to get on the second level of the career ladder.

Q. Let me get this straight. I heard you say earlier that if a teacher is lacking, you may need to think of termination. But is there any kind of typical scenario in which the teacher and the principal together develop some kind of growth plan for that teacher?

A. Right! Almost all of the time in evaluation what we are trying to do is to improve the level of instruction. If things are not working out, you keep on recommending. 'This is what we need to do – let's work together and find out what we can do – I'm going to go into the classroom and watch you – let me present a lesson and you watch me and see what I do.' We are always aiming for improvement; but if it does not come, that's another matter.

A young classroom teacher in one state, asked what she thought was the objective of the appraisal process answered succinctly: 'State law'. On her right of appeal if she received an appraisal with which she was dissatisfied she was positively cynical: 'We can refuse to sign, but then they could very well refuse to hire you again too. Without this form being presented to the Board ·of Education they will not rehire you.' She has some healthy criticism of the grading system in use in her district: 'The highest level is "appropriate level of performance". I think I would go along with it better if I could see "excellent", "good", "satisfactory". "Room for growth", it says; tell me about a teacher who does not have room for growth.' Nevertheless, despite these misgivings, she is enthusiastic about the appraisal process and regards the classroom observations as helpful in the identification of areas for improvement and the development of growth plans.

CONCLUSION

What happens in the USA, valuable in that it is based on a much longer experience of appraisal than we have in this country, serves mainly to identify that their original aims were widely at variance from ours. This is not to say that there was not a strong element of personal and professional improvement in the appraisal processes devised by most states, but rather that there was an excessive concern with summative outcomes. For educators in the USA that has not been without cost.

> The net result of these pressures for more careful summative judgments of teachers is to put administrators under particular strain. Though 'better' performance evaluation may appear to make the issues explicit and decisions objective, it may also generate as much heat as light, particularly where the various constituents to the design of evaluation do not agree. The pressure to improve teaching performance may foster more elaborate evaluation systems, but with summative thrusts getting in the way of formative efforts.
>
> (Knapp, 1982)

Though the thoroughness with which Boards of Education have analysed and listed teaching competencies and performance criteria is exemplary, there is nevertheless an element there of overcomplexity of which we must beware as we move towards any similar analyses. Furthermore:

> it is one thing to devise and measure teacher competence in a standardized fashion; it is quite another to change teacher performance . . . The context-free generalization necessary for implementing a uniform evaluation system may counteract the context-specific processes needed to effect change in individual or organizational behaviors.
>
> (Darling-Hammond et al., 1983)

It is good to have firsthand evidence that state regulations do not preclude the addition to state performance criteria of district-specific and even school-specific criteria. In the face of strong pressures from central government in the UK for education to move towards conformity, it is helpful to remind ourselves that appraisal processes need to operate within the organisational system of each school and not be subject to some abstract notion of what that system might or ought to be. It would be a sad day for education in the UK if we were to move away from guidelines, which can be helpful to schools in establishing their own processes for appraisal as for any other innovation, to regulations which tie schools to imposed systems.

We need also to learn from the US experience that the appraisal processes will be largely dictated by the concept of *cui bono?* As Darling-Hammond and her colleagues succinctly put it, 'external demands for accountability are at odds with internal organizational needs for stability and trust'; and again:

> [Different] stakeholders have divergent views on the primary purpose of teacher evaluation . . . Teachers have a stake in maintaining their jobs, their self-respect and their sense of efficacy. Parents and public officials . . . want in general an evaluation system that relates teacher performance to teacher effectiveness.
>
> (Darling-Hammond *et al.*, 1983)

Of particular importance as we look at teacher appraisal in the USA is the effect of concern, whether justified or merely supposed, about termination of tenure. Those who use market force and incentive arguments for the introduction of limited tenure teaching contracts in the UK, and who see appraisal as a means of evaluating whether or not to re-employ, might do well to take note of the way in which appraisal processes on the other side of the Atlantic have been influenced by rating procedures, by attempts, that is, to establish criteria whereby one teacher can be reliably said to be more effective than another. It is far from certain whether appraisal, as used there, does in fact identify the effective teacher:

> Teacher evaluation has become an increasingly rule-based process, linked less to judgments of competence than to evidence about whether teachers have adhered to clearly specified minimum work standards.
>
> (Darling-Hammond *et al.*, 1983)

We have always held that the professional competency of any individual member of staff is a concern for the school staff as a whole and for those in managerial roles in particular; that our task as educationists is not to weed out the incompetent but constantly to aid all teachers to reach the highest level of competency of which they are capable. The firsthand experience of which we have heard suggests that this same principle is operative in many schools in the USA. Nevertheless, because of the considerable stress that is laid on documentation using scales of assessment legislated by states and districts, it is in principle fundamentally summative.

One concern we undoubtedly share with transatlantic school administrators is that of the lack of time for appraisal. All school principals and assistant principals with whom we have spoken or from whom we have heard either complain that they are under considerable pressure to conduct appraisals as laid down or admit to cutting corners. In those states whose legislation we have most closely studied, the frequency of classroom observation and of appraisal interviews has been cut back from the initial propositions. We have already seen evidence in the UK, in schools which have developed their own appraisal processes rather than in those within the LEA pilot schemes where there was an element of financial and logistical support, that time costs are seen as a major obstacle to an effective system. Even within the pilot schemes there is reported evidence (Arkin, 1989) that appraisal often takes longer than the time allocated to it: 'Ashburton [High School in Croydon] allocates eight hours a year contact time for each appraisal but in practice the process often takes longer and eats into teachers' own time'.

We should not let the differences of culture, climate and perhaps of intended outcomes blind us to the thoroughness with which appraisal has been developed in the USA with resources invested in establishing, trialling and disseminating appraisal processes that we are unlikely to match. In many states these processes have, as they have evolved, been shared with principals and teachers. In all the states from which we have evidence the amount of time and money spent in training appraisers – and in regularly updating that training – makes the sums so far set aside by the DES seem paltry and totally inadequate for the task. Although our appraisal processes must reflect our needs and our culture, we would be foolish not to take cognisance of the extensive transatlantic experience.

Chapter 4

Appraisal: tertiary education

The suggestion of the Prices and Incomes Board in 1968 that the teaching of lecturers should be appraised was part of a growing movement to increase their accountability, and to attempt to measure the 'value for money' provided by lecturing staff. At the same time the need for more systematic training of lecturers was recognised and systems of staff development, mainly for the purpose of induction, began to appear. By the 1970s, of approximately thirty polytechnics, no more than six had staff development programmes that included an interview to identify training needs. By the end of the 1970s it remained true that: 'appraisal systems . . . are still rare in colleges. Colleges have put much energy into creating and improving staff development systems, but that is quite another thing' (Turner, 1981).

By 1985 most polytechnics had a policy on staff development which included provision for a so-called staff appraisal − by which was meant an interview of some kind which reviewed the previous year's work and perhaps identified training needs − applicable to lecturers rather than heads of department or the directorate. In the same year 65 per cent of agricultural colleges were planning or had installed similar staff development schemes. As part of the pay deal for lecturers, universities were in 1987 required to install and maintain a system of performance appraisal. In few universities, and in some of those few in some departments only, had there been any previous system of appraisal; consequently in the years that followed they have been much involved in learning about and experiencing the process. Bath University is one of the very few which have had sufficient experience to warrant a review of the system in operation there and to report on lessons that have been learned.

In tertiary education, therefore, experience over the years has been patchy. Some valuable studies have been undertaken and are referred to later in this chapter. However, one must be cautious in making deductions from this evidence. In the first place, the schemes are too new for any long-term evaluations to have been conducted; and secondly, because each scheme must be appropriate to the culture and history of that organisation, there is no guarantee that what has been learnt will be readily transferable. One example to illustrate this will suffice. When an appraisal scheme was being negotiated by the staff of one tertiary institution, it was initially decided that there should be a third party present at the appraisal interview. This was a place where there had previously been much concern over apparent nepotism and prejudice. Other institutions without such suspicions undoubtedly preferred a duologue which would emphasise confidentiality and the strengthening of a relationship between the interviewer and the interviewee.

PRESSURES FOR APPRAISAL

The general situation in polytechnics and colleges as they entered the 1990s was one of flux, with a dispute over pay and conditions of service hampering the introduction of appraisal schemes. At the same time, however, many of these institutions were quietly laying the groundwork for the introduction of appraisal, partly in the hope that a prepared scheme which met staff requirements might well be viewed favourably by their funding bodies and the institutions' own governors. If they waited, they feared that they would have foisted on them an unattractive scheme.

Many enquiries were being received by one of the lecturers' unions, the National Association of Teachers in Further and Higher Education (NATFHE), for union guidelines or advice on how to set up a suitable scheme. The union accepted the case for the introduction of a system of appraisal. Nevertheless, it was discouraging its members from setting up schemes independently before collective agreement had been reached, for fear that a proliferation of schemes throughout the country would make a concerted approach to the institutions' paymasters more difficult. Thus, in early 1990, in polytechnics and colleges there was as yet no generally agreed pattern. The nature of both staff development systems and the type of appraisal varied from one institution to another, and even within institutions or within the same department.

Pressure towards the setting up of staff development systems which include performance appraisal comes not only from outside the institution but also from within. Polytechnics and colleges have many lecturers with experience in industry, and therefore with experience of industrial appraisal systems, who have expectations of feedback from their line managers. Occasionally such individuals have naively asked for interviews with their heads of department. 'How am I doing?' they have demanded to know. The standard reply, which can be summed up as 'I have heard no complaints so you must be doing all right', they did not find very satisfactory! It is widely held, in all walks of life, that individuals have the right to know what assessments are being made of their work by their employers. Assessments there certainly are; but, when covert, they are far more likely to be based on prejudice, impulse, incorrect or incomplete information, or the more recent or dramatic events that have occurred. Assessments, it is argued, could be made more objective, and less influenced by show, special pleading and the like, if they were incorporated into a formal appraisal system, based on objective data and assessed by overt criteria.

One of the early pressures for the introduction of appraisal schemes was the desire for accountability, to 'weed out' below par lecturers, to ensure that the public was getting value for money. Thus there was a hard, judgmental, even punitive approach to appraisal. Such an approach might possibly work adequately in an organisation which does not require the exercise of independent judgment and initiative, but is unlikely to obtain the type of commitment required from lecturers. If a judgmental appraisal scheme were to be introduced, the relationship between appraiser and appraisee would tend to become unilateral, coercive and supervisory; the interviewee who felt coerced might comply, but probably the amount of voluntary effort and creativity would diminish. Perhaps for these reasons it is now more widely accepted that the judgmental approach is inappropriate: management has the power to use disciplinary procedures to weed out, if necessary; and it can also use selection, induction and staff development to improve the quality of the teaching. Appraisal within a staff development system can be used primarily as the means of encouraging professional development, and all tertiary sector appraisal schemes which we have studied are concerned with staff development not judgmental appraisal.

WHAT SHOULD BE REVIEWED?

In tertiary education, many lecturers spend less time in front of a class than on a wide range of other activities: academic research in their specialism; course administration, monitoring and evaluation; student research and placement supervision; the development of new courses and materials. The appraisal of any such lecturer needs therefore to include a review and forecast of such activities, and the identification of training needs in those areas as well as in teaching.

Schools today have a comparable range of managerial, administrative and developmental activities. While teaching will always be an important element of any teacher's job, the management of the educational process also occupies time, and the proportion of time spent on teaching tends to decrease as the teacher moves up the organisation's hierarchy. Newcomers to teaching may not recognise the managerial elements of their jobs, regarding it as an essential but indistinguishable part of teaching; but to be effective they must manage time and resources and must plan, organise and control their own work and that of the students. Progression to more senior positions involves the coordination, supervision and management of the work of peers within a department or throughout a school. At all levels of education, therefore, the non-teaching element of the job should also be included in the review of every teacher's work.

In tertiary education the most common procedure for the staff development review or performance appraisal is to invite interviewees to prepare for the interview by self-assessment, that is, to review for themselves under a number of headings the work of the previous year. In private sector appraisal schemes a clear job specification is provided for each member of staff and the appraisal is made against it. However, in tertiary education there are many lecturers who have no job specification or, at best, one very vaguely worded. This is not entirely due to the slackness of management; it is also a consequence of the complexity and changing nature of the lecturer's job, a change that will accelerate. The late 1980s have seen the development of new types of employment in which the narrowly defined job specification no longer seems appropriate. In academic organisations, and particularly in polytechnics, many members of staff are now having to take on *ad hoc* non-teaching responsibilities, often of considerable importance to the institution, that do not easily fit into a predetermined job specification.

APPRAISING TEACHING PERFORMANCE IN TERTIARY INSTITUTIONS

The amount of a lecturer's time that is allocated to administration, industrial liaison, course management, research and other non-teaching duties is usually greater than that allocated to comparable non-teaching activities in schools. Nevertheless, teaching is still an important element in the work of most lecturers. Accordingly, where appraisal schemes exist, it is the practice to make some form of assessment of teaching performance, though, as yet, this assessment is still superficial and informal.

In the twenty years or so since the assessment of lecturers' teaching performance was suggested by the Prices and Incomes Board, a considerable amount of research has been carried out in this country and much reference made to the experience of similar institutions in North America. During the 1970s the Council for National Academic Awards (CNAA) kept the issue alive by its requirements for course monitoring and evaluation, one of which was for student representation on course management committees. Interest in the subject was further stimulated in 1987 with the requirement that university lecturers accept appraisal, and the general acceptance by other elements of tertiary education that they too would be required to adopt staff appraisal. Much of the debate about key issues and research carried out during the 1970s is relevant and is valid today; but now there is a stronger political will to enforce on lecturers what some have felt to be an additional burden.

Most lecturers accept that, if there is to be appraisal, then in principle teaching should be included. Yet there remains an uneasiness about the validity of the process. Although not frequently articulated, it may well be based on a number of valid objections to the assumptions underlying the process.

The first assumption is that there is merit in measuring teaching effectiveness. In business it is becoming increasingly common that managers agree goals with their subordinates and then allow them to achieve these goals in whatever way they think fit. Instead of spending time appraising style, procedures and activities, the manager will review the employee's success in achieving goals. Only if there is a shortfall between achievement and objectives will it be necessary to review the methods used.

In lecturing, the main objective is not to put on a performance, but to promote learning of some kind. It could therefore be argued that the main focus of the appraiser's attention should be directed towards the students' learning achievements rather than to the lecturer's classroom behaviour; only when students fail should teaching be appraised. Nevertheless, there are clearly some weaknesses in this argument:

- good learning does not necessarily indicate that no improvements in the teaching are desirable; students can learn in spite of their lecturers, and can even overcome difficulties put in their way;
- although learning is the main objective, student enjoyment and satisfaction is also an important goal, and measures of learning do not indicate levels of satisfaction. Some enquiry into student satisfaction as well as student learning is desirable.

Again, while it is easy to assess student ability to regurgitate information in examinations, it may not be feasible to assess the really important learning that occurs: the sudden insights, the creative extrapolation, the new perspectives and independent judgments that students form as they argue, read or write essays. Hence all the intended outcomes of teaching cannot be measured. Monitoring of teaching, and the continual improvement of teaching, are not possible by focusing only on the primary outcome of student learning.

Student involvement in staff appraisal?

One important element in tertiary staff appraisal is assessment of performance. This, whether made by the students themselves or by an observer, is usually referred to as *feedback*. It can provide valuable information to lecturers on how recipients of their teaching react to their methods and style of delivery. To be effective this feedback must be prompt if it is to consolidate or change behaviours.

It is interesting to note that, when teachers were rated on a thirty-eight item questionnaire in the USA, researchers (Gromisch, 1972; Sagan, 1974) found no correlation between the judgments of students and observers. If observers and students do not reliably agree on assessment, whose opinion should be sought? A frequent reply is that, since students are consumers of instruction, they should be the ones to judge it. This view, together with the problem of bias in a single rater, has led to teacher assessment in the USA being based on student ratings.

In tertiary education, feedback is generally obtained by asking students to fill in a form. Figure 4.1 illustrates a 'free-response' type of questionnaire, consisting of simple questions and space for comment. A second type of form consists of twenty to forty questions to which the students respond by ticking boxes, as in an objective test. The more complex forms have the advantage that they direct students' attention to certain points that they might otherwise have overlooked. More importantly, perhaps, they remind lecturers of important teaching techniques: clear chalkboard work, for example, or audible delivery. The main problem with these complex questionnaires is that they represent the constructor's opinions of what behaviours promote good teaching.

There will be general agreement about the need for clarity of expression, good use of resources and warm and friendly relationships with students. Thereafter there is less agreement. Students from different disciplines have different priorities and requirements. Research by Ramsden (1975), for example, reveals that in England arts and social science students value a teacher's sensitivity significantly more than do science and engineering students. On the other hand, it is more important to science students than to arts students that the lecturer proceeds at a suitable pace for the class to take notes. Clearly, one teaching assessment form is not universally appropriate. Again, it is arguable that the art of teaching is individualistic, determined as much by the personality of lecturers as by their skills and knowledge. Standard assessment forms are unlikely to elicit responses applicable to the particular teaching style of the individual teacher. What is true of the tertiary education lecturer faced with a largely homogeneous class is even more true of the primary or secondary teacher dealing with a wide range of ability.

A further problem with the use of the standard questionnaire is that its use will tend to reduce experimentation in new forms of delivery and education. For, if lecturers were to believe they were to be assessed against a standard set of performance criteria, they may well be constrained to improve their performance against these criteria rather than to explore alternative ways forward.

Classroom observation?

Another method of obtaining data about a person's teaching ability is classroom observation where a head of department, professional tutor or

Figure 4.1 Free-response questionnaire

STUDENT FEEDBACK

I would like you to give me, anonymously, your opinions on the teaching of the session/course. Your views are valuable in helping to improve teaching.

What was good about the teaching/course?

What was less satisfactory?

In what ways could the teaching/course be improved?

© Routledge 1991

other member of staff observes a lecturer in the classroom. This practice already exists in tertiary education, but, with rare exceptions, only for new lecturers during their probationary period. The time cost of regular observations would have to be accounted for in tertiary institutions against other, probably revenue-producing activities that the observer might engage in; and the negative attitudes to their introduction by the majority of experienced staff do not offer much promise for its further use in tertiary education as an element in appraisal.

If the purpose of observation is to rate a teacher's effectiveness, it is argued, then inevitably the subjective approach of the observer will lead to problems: the rating may be affected by a personal bias toward leniency or severity; by the 'halo effect', whereby an overall favourable impression or the presence of one favourable characteristic affects the observer's judgment of other characteristics; or by the observer's preference for a particular style of teaching. Such biases are likely to affect the quality of the feedback given to the teacher, and consequently the validity of any assessment. To overcome this problem checklists and questionnaires which encourage objectivity might be adopted, with their attendant problems.

A second issue is that of the comparability of ratings made by different observers. If the data were to be used only to provide feedback to teachers, then the issue of comparability would not arise; but were classroom observation to be used to compare the teaching ability of several internal candidates for promotion or the award of merit pay then obviously comparability of the observation of different observers is of paramount importance.

Where raters make quantitative judgments of large numbers of staff, it is possible to derive a statistical measure of their biases and to adjust ratings and assessments to achieve comparability. Within an educational institution, however, it is unlikely that any one person will assess more than a few cases and hence it will be impossible to correlate response biases.

While there is a tenable case for the use of standard scales for student assessment of teachers, the weight of the evidence is, in the opinion of experienced observers, against their use. Standard scales are constrictive and do not make use of the skills of the expert. The expert observer can draw on a wide range of experience and knowledge of the probable factors determining the effectiveness of delivery in a particular classroom, lecture theatre or workshop at a given time. In part the observer acts as a sensitive instrument, responding to the teacher's initiatives and sensing the reactions of the students. The questionnaire or standard checklist cannot adjust its weightings to the situation, add or delete questions as appropriate and above all cannot make suggestions as to alternative teaching strategies appropriate to the particular teacher, topic or class. The checklist or questionnaire may provide a useful *aide memoire* for the observer, but the responses to its items will be of less value to the lecturer than the professional judgment of an observer.

THE FINDINGS OF RESEARCH STUDIES

Alternative approaches to the assessment of teacher effectiveness have been explored in a study in which a tutor sought to discover the success of his teaching by measuring the achievement of his objectives. Boud and Turner (1974) abandoned the attempt to measure the effectiveness of teaching by judging the quality of the presentation, and replaced it by individually constructed scales intended to measure how well the lecturer achieved his chosen objectives. The two authors drew up a list of objectives for a course taught by one of them. They then asked the students the following questions:

- In an ideal course, how far are these objectives desirable?
- How far are they seen to be the objectives of the present course?
- Are the objectives being achieved?
- Do you think they will be examined?

The study demonstrated that there were some wide differences between the students' perceptions of the objectives of an ideal course and the extent to which these objectives were being achieved on this course. The study was found to be a useful method for uncovering problem areas in a course. Unfortunately these pioneering studies do not necessarily provide a direction forward for the appraisal of teaching: they are time-consuming, require elaborate analysis and do not provide clues as to what the lecturer might do to resolve the problems uncovered by the research. Furthermore, this approach makes the assumption that the tutor, not the student, should invariably set the objectives for the course.

The growing view in many fields of tertiary education, and especially in management education and training, is that the student is well able to set his own learning objectives, at least for parts of his learning. In independent learning groups, learning communities and similar learning circles the participants are responsible for setting their own learning goals, devising ways for learning from their peers and from resources, selecting methods of learning and proposing methods of assessment. In such situations the appraisal of the teacher cannot follow approaches appropriate to the teaching of a large group of students studying for an externally examined professional course, but must use a battery of techniques appropriate to these newer forms of study.

It follows therefore that there are dangers inherent in using standard methods of gathering data on teaching performance. This is not to suggest that consequently the attempt should be abandoned, but that awareness of some of the problems might help to prevent excessive reliance being placed in these measures. This view was put thus by Ron Shepherd, a guest speaker from industry at a national education conference:

> All I think that we would claim is that, at best, any personnel appraisal system has inherent weaknesses which mean that it can be no more than an aid to good management. It certainly cannot in any way be a substitute for it. In other words, as long as one knows the limitations of the tool being used, it can still be better than having no tool at all. That is as much, at this stage, as one can claim for that.
>
> (AMMA, 1988)

Some of the findings of research into appraisal schemes in polytechnics, especially those of Bayter (1989), have general applicability. Bayter studied the introduction of performance appraisal among librarians in polytechnics and found that interviewees had wide-ranging mixed feelings towards the proposal to introduce appraisal – from cynicism to support – but no downright hostility. Initial feelings depended partly on the level of trust, respect for and confidence in management. Interviewees felt that among the benefits of a regular staff development interview was the opportunity to talk to management and to express feelings about the job. Some of the negative feelings included:

- a fear that confidential information would be made public;
- suspicions of the value of the scheme if there were no resources for training, and no follow-up;
- doubts about the value of the scheme in cases where good communication and good relationships already existed;
- fears that appraisal might adversely affect career prospects.

Interviewees were later asked about the benefits and problems they had experienced after schemes had been implemented. These included:

- the chance for staff to talk and to express their views, particularly valuable for those who feel unwilling or unable to communicate;
- the provision of a formal, recognised and confidential opportunity to say what one needs to say, in a situation which would carry more weight than an informal chat;
- the provision of an opportunity to discuss problems before they become crises.

Interviewers believed that the main benefit to staff was the opportunity individually to discuss work and future prospects. Interviews were held to be valuable but the real benefit to the organisation came from the follow-up of agreed action plans. The follow-up also confirmed to staff the relevance of the staff development interview.

The main problem is the perceived – and actual – lack of resources to fulfil training plans and to hold effective follow-up reviews. Naturally both sides will become disappointed with a system which merely identifies but does not correct weaknesses, which promises but does not supply training, or which has insufficient resources to monitor and encourage the achievement of targets agreed at the interview.

When questioned about their experience of the staff development interview, staff preferred, so Bayter discovered, a formal approach with a structured agenda so that they knew what to expect and could prepare for it. Not surprisingly, they preferred firm target-setting and planned follow-up to an open-ended, unspecific approach. Some concern was felt about the accessibility and ownership of records of interviews.

Bayter found that unless the appraisal system met the needs of the organisation, the department and the individual members of staff it would fail through lack of support. Interviewees felt that appraisal should be developmental not judgmental and consequently should focus on the present and future rather than on past mistakes. It was felt that the interview should not be related to reward or promotion. Some of Bayter's further recommendations are that the staff development interview:

- should focus on performance not personality;
- should accommodate individual needs by providing a choice of interviewers in cases where there might be prejudice or favouritism;
- while judgments may be qualitative, indicators of performance should be as firm and precise as possible;
- the interview must be a two-way process: communication between people, not one instructing or informing another;
- the experience of conducting a staff developmental interview is itself a developmental act for the interviewer, and consequently it is expedient to involve more rather than fewer interviewers;
- training is required not only for appraisers, but also for appraisees to enable them to make the best possible use of the staff development interview;
- it is important to emphasise to both interviewers and interviewees the importance of preparation for the interview by reviewing the previous year's work in the light of the job specification and the record of previous interviews.

Bayter also argues that, as in any other innovation, pilot studies beforehand and monitoring and evaluation reviews after implementation are desirable. She concludes that appraisal can be either a force for positive personal and organisational growth or a source of frustration and a meaningless exercise. What it becomes depends on the context and climate; and there must be trust between and commitment from all those involved.

The effects of a successfully run appraisal scheme are a greater openness and honesty and the promotion of individual and organisational objectives. The approach to work is sharpened and employees develop in confidence and competence. Heads of department are forced to think of their staff as individuals and to get to know them better; two-way communication is opened, problems are discussed freely and more frequently solved satisfactorily.

Chapter 5

Classroom performance

If appraisal is to have school improvement as its main concern, then it follows that what teachers spend most of their time engaged in – involving their pupils in the learning process, otherwise known as teaching – must be a central feature of the appraisal process. Classroom observation reveals 'a view of the climate, rapport, interaction and functioning of the classroom available from no other source' (Evertson and Holley, 1981). It is an essential feature of staff development. Not only is it valuable in its own right, as a vehicle for one-to-one in-service education and the sharing of ideas within the school on teaching content and methodology; it also is vital in order to ensure that both the goalsetting and the interview elements of appraisal relate, not to abstractions, but to what is for most teachers the key element of their role.

Teachers have grown used in the past decade to a welter of distractions from the main purpose of the profession. Innovation after innovation has taken them out of the classroom, both physically and in spirit, so that they have become preoccupied with managerial issues, either as part of their role or because they seem likely to affect their role profoundly. Difficult though it may at times be to maintain a hold on this perception, for most teachers, for most of their working day, the preparation and conduct of lessons is their crucial concern.

Yet the teaching profession as a whole remains very uneasy about classroom observation for many reasons, some well founded, some questionable. The appraisal of classroom performance will sit uncomfortably on the shoulders of appraisers and appraisees alike unless and until these reservations are brought into the open.

First, it has to be accepted that we have a long tradition of the autonomy of the classroom. This stems in part from the growth, quite rightly, of the concept that the teacher is a professional and that professions are self-regulating. The work of doctors, it is argued, is not overseen once they have completed their qualifications and their postgraduate experiential training; nor that of solicitors and lawyers when they have completed their pupillage. Yet this comparison is flawed. The medical and legal professions provide opportunities for intra-professional dialogue about their clients at a level which is denied to teachers. Furthermore, their relationship with clients is on a one-to-one basis. The teacher, in contrast, has to engage both with the individual pupil and with that indeterminate unit that we call a class: 'indeterminate' because it has come into being by the sheer chance of age, ability and aptitude in any combination that the school's policy dictates. Until very recently, one might hear the observation, made with a curious mixture of pride and criticism: 'In our profession it is possible, once one has passed one's probation, to go right through to retirement without ever once having one's teaching observed'.

It is a consequence, too, of the physical structure of the majority of our schools. Open-plan school buildings, however one cares to define the concept, provide opportunities for teachers to see what their colleagues are doing, to share experiences, to engage in peer criticism in an unthreatening way and in general to develop a corporate approach to the teaching process. Yet, in spite of the many advances made in school architecture, a majority of teachers are still teaching in classroom cells, effectively insulated from their colleagues, either because so many are teaching in schools which were designed and built long ago or because in some cases they have, in more modern buildings, physically or psychologically recreated the isolation in which they feel more comfortable.

Secondly, there is the argument put forward in some schools that headteachers – and, in secondary schools, senior and middle management – are 'in and out of classrooms all the time anyway'. While undoubtedly the ready acceptance by pupils and staff alike that classrooms are not restricted domains or no-go areas will facilitate classroom observation for teacher appraisal, it is important that a clear distinction is made between the casual and the structured observation. Both are integral to the appraisal process, but the former is not an acceptable alternative for the latter:

> The old methods of walking through classrooms or occasionally shadowing the timetable of a particular teaching group are a poor substitute for the rigour of a structured attempt to improve the learning of pupils and the professional development of staff.
>
> (Moran, 1990)

What this practice may well do, however, is to mitigate the effect of 'the stranger in our midst', for both teacher and class, that the presence of the classroom observer implies. This is the third, and certainly most cogent reservation that the teaching profession has about classroom observation. There are, it is true, many open access and community schools in which the presence in the classroom of adults other than the class teacher goes unnoticed by the pupils; but even here the presence of another teacher, whether peer or senior, for a full lesson, possibly taking notes and certainly present in a capacity not readily recognised as 'normal' will make a difference. Some pupils will react by playing to the gallery, others by becoming unusually reticent, to the extent that highly competent teachers may well end up by wondering what on earth was wrong with that lesson that it should have produced such atypical responses.

It is not only the class that may react in this way. Some teachers may feel impelled to 'put on a show' and, in so doing, they are likely to achieve a lesson of far less merit than had they viewed their observation lesson not as a performance on which they were being judged, but as an occasion on which, as far as possible, they would be demonstrating their normal day-to-day skills. There is ample evidence from schools which have been engaged for some years in classroom observation as a part of appraisal trialling that teachers and pupils alike soon begin to adapt without difficulty to what has in the past been for most of them an exceptional experience.

Nevertheless, it is important to recognise that there will always be an element of stress for both pupils and teacher in the classroom observation process. The status of the observer and the importance of the occasion will be the main reasons for this. There are those who argue that the unheralded visit will both ensure that the lesson is a natural one and relieve tension. This we very much doubt. There are many occasions during the school week when a lesson may be low-key but still effective; but our experience tells us that, caught unawares as it will seem to them, teachers will assume that a high profile stance is expected of them and take up a centre-stage position. The situation will then become unreal for the teacher, the class and, indeed, the observer. There is every reason for headteachers and their senior curricular and pastoral staff to visit classrooms as often as their many other duties allow, but it would be erroneous to confuse this casual activity with that of formal classroom observation. If appraisal is to be an experience in which there is trust and mutuality, then the classroom observation element must have a structure which encourages open behaviour, is unambiguous in its intended outcomes and seeks to promote in the teacher the confidence to perform at the highest possible level.

BRIEFING FOR CLASSROOM OBSERVATION

The briefing session should take place at least one day before the lesson which is being observed, in a place and atmosphere in which both observer and teacher can feel at ease. It is likely to take from 15 to 30 minutes and therefore half an hour should be set aside for the activity. The lesson notes need to be in the hands of the observer well in advance of the meeting, at least the day before.

Establishing the context

Every lesson depends for its content and methodology on what has preceded

Figure 5.1 Briefing for classroom observation

BEFORE THE LESSON

- Establish the context

- Ascertain the teacher's aims and expectations

- Share the lesson plan

- Identify potential difficulties and constraints

- Agree the observation style

- Agree the focus

- Contract for debriefing

© Routledge 1991

---

it and what is intended to succeed it: it is part of a teaching/learning continuum. The observer therefore needs to learn from the class teacher where in that continuum the lesson stands. Most observers, whether they are senior managers or heads of department/curriculum coordinators, will already have an awareness of the broad context of the lesson, either through lesson preparation notes which they routinely see or from the minutes of departmental or team meetings. That knowledge is, however, too general to make this stage of the briefing process superfluous. Moreover, because it lies within the ownership of the class teacher, discussion enables rapport and confidence to be more readily established.

For early years teachers and in schools which operate the integrated day, the term 'lesson' must be given a wide interpretation. It is no less important that there be a mutual understanding of what is expected to take place during the period of time set aside for the observation; but greater flexibility and improvisation must be expected and, indeed, looked for. What the observer will see is 'a slice of the moving river'. Where there is a wide range of activities taking place, the observer will naturally need to choose between wide sampling – that is taking a brief look at as many activities as possible – and narrow sampling – looking more intensively at fewer activities.

Ascertaining aims and expectations

Again, the purpose of this area of the briefing process is to ensure that the teacher is being observed in the light of his intended outcomes and not those assumed by the observer. Wragg (1987) trenchantly points out that 'the art of constructive observation is to . . . concentrate on helping the teacher'. This is best done by obtaining through discussion – and then maintaining throughout the observation – the teacher's perspective on the lesson. Whether the observer might have had different aims and expectations is largely irrelevant. Alternative approaches in methodology, other ideas about content, are of course worth sharing between colleagues but to do so at this particular time would be destructive of a teacher's confidence and would raise questions about the ownership of the lesson.

We have often been asked in training workshops whether, if the observer perceives at this stage that the aims and expectations are inappropriate for the class being observed, an intervention is permissible. The judgment called for here is to distinguish in advance between a lesson in which mistakes will be made but which will still be a valuable learning experience for the teacher and one which even now appears to be signalling the possibility of breakdown. Certainly, in teasing out with a teacher what the aims and expectations of the lesson are, the observer may well disclose that there are some aspects of the plan over which she has reservations. One does not behave like Jove on Olympus, dispassionately watching puny man falter and stumble. Nevertheless, it is for the teacher, not the observer, to decide whether or not the plan should be modified in the light of the discussion.

Sharing the lesson plan

First, let it be taken for granted that the lesson plan which the teacher produces for the observation lesson is likely to be more thoroughly prepared and more detailed than the normal lesson preparation. Tactful enquiries we have made from time to time over the past three years indicate that in many schools – particularly secondary – the requirement that all teachers hand in lesson preparation notes at the beginning of the week has fallen into desuetude, except for teachers in their period of probation, when it is required of them. This is not surprising, in view of the increased pressure on senior staff. With so many changes imposed on the profession by the Education (No.2) Act 1986 and the Education Reform Act 1988, something has to give. We find a sad contradiction between the Government's ardent desire for better standards of classroom performance and its denial to schools, through overload, of one simple but effective way of promoting dialogue on content and methodology.

Nevertheless, regardless of how many years they have been teaching, teachers do continue to prepare their lessons, though rarely in such detail as that on page 56. It must be recognised that, however hard the observer has worked to defuse the tensions that are bound to arise and to establish an atmosphere of normality for lesson observation, the situation is *not* normal; and teachers must be excused if they treat the occasion as exceptional and make exceptional preparation for it.

We believe it to be helpful if the lesson plan is in written form. This makes sure that there is a common understanding of the content of the lesson and enables the observer to prepare in advance of the briefing. However, an excellent sequence in one of the pilot LEA training videos (see Appendix 2) shows the Head of the Infant Department of a Somerset school talking through the lesson plan with her appraiser while he takes notes. It may be that experienced and senior teachers will be more comfortable with the more informal approach and those whose memories of their teacher training and probationary days are not so distant less put out by having to present a written outline.

It must be emphasised that the lesson plan, like the aims and expectations, is in the ownership of the teacher. The observer's main objective is to ensure that she has a full understanding of what it is that the teacher is expecting to happen in the lesson in fulfilment of his aims and expectations. Good teachers are responsive to stimuli from their pupils, and it should not be in the minds of either party that the plan is a rigid measuring rod against which the success or failure of the lesson will be judged.

Classroom observation: secondary lesson notes

English lesson, year 8: mixed ability class, 29 on roll. The 40 minute lesson is part of a six-week project on newspapers. Previous lessons have dealt with advertising (one single and two doubles); the proportion of space devoted to news items compared with finance, sport, features, cartoons, TV and radio, etc. (two single lessons, one homework); survey of newspaper readership habits (one single, one double lesson, one homework).

OBJECTIVES
- To promote awareness of the different reporting styles of a variety of daily newspapers.
- To encourage the ability to discriminate between fact and opinion, and to identify bias, inference and emotive language.

PREPARATION
Photocopies of one article on the same topic from six newspapers: *Sun*, *Daily Mail*, *Independent*, *Guardian*, *Mirror*, *Today*.

LESSON PLAN
Introduction (10 minutes): recap on findings so far – explain objectives of this lesson – introduce with OHP of different headline treatment of same (imaginary) event.

In groups (20 minutes): distribute sets of photocopied articles.

Pupils individually, for 5 minutes, read articles.
NB: Each member of group to read *at least one* article in this time. No discussion at this stage.

Groupwork, for 15 minutes, following tasks (cyclostyled sheet per group) presented in the form of questions e.g. Can you find . . .?

- one *fact* and to check that it is reported consistently in all six papers.
- one *opinion* and to see if this is shared by all six papers.
- six instances of the use of *emotive language* from any of the papers. Compare two or more papers if possible.
- if possible, *one* instance of inference and *one* of bias.
- if time, to put articles in rank order for *factual presentation* and also for *readability* and compare the two rank orders.

Plenary: compare group findings.

© Routledge 1991

The teacher should talk through the plan, with questions by the observer designed to ensure that she has a full understanding of what is proposed. Some of the questions will arise from the observer's interest in the plan: How were the six newspapers chosen? What is the topic that you have selected for comparison of treatment in these newspapers? How were the groups formed? Were the group leaders elected or selected?

There may be other questions in the mind of the observer that may need to be asked: How accustomed are the children to working in groups? Have you made any contingency plans, with this tight time scheme, to cover the possibility that the final element of the plan will not be reached? What follows this activity?

Potential difficulties and constraints

From these last questions there follows naturally the identification of problems that might arise in the course of the lesson about which the observer might helpfully be apprised. Every class has its Fearsome Freddie (or Freda) who *may* be cooperative because the observer is present but is just as likely to use the occasion to be highly disruptive. If the observer is very senior, both the class and the teacher may look to her to deal with the incident. It is as well for the teacher and the observer to have established an agreed policy on who is to be responsible for class control. It must surely be the class teacher, save in exceptional circumstances.

There will be times when the teacher will seize the opportunity to raise more general matters which present difficulties: lack of resources, unsatisfactory accommodation, pupils with special needs that are not being adequately catered for. These should not be dismissed by the observer as irrelevant to the lesson observation. For one thing, they are not irrelevant from the point of view of the teacher, and that is what matters. For another, a few minutes spent listening may reveal to the observer aspects of school management that she might improve or alternatively make known to staff who are in a position to act upon them.

For teachers who are unused to being observed, this element of the briefing process will prove most useful in reinforcing the concept that class observation is not intended to be judgmental, but is concerned with school improvement as much as with teacher performance. In the early years of appraisal, and for some teachers possibly for quite a long time after, there will be unease, misconception and sometimes downright cynicism about the process. Time spent in dialogue will rarely be time wasted.

Agreeing observation style

Fly on the wall or co-teacher? These are not so much alternatives as extremes of a spectrum within which the teacher and observer will identify the desired observation style. Highly experienced observers – HMI, university researchers, LEA advisers – may have the skill to become 'part of the furniture' within a classroom. For those whom the class will recognise as teachers within their own school but who appear to be wearing, exceptionally, a different hat, this kind of anonymity is not easily achieved. In a teacher-centred lesson, it is more likely that the observer will soon be absorbed into the class: watching, at pupil level as it were, a demonstration science experiment, a video or a film; or listening to a story which leads to questions and answers from the class. In an activity lesson like the one being considered, it is not merely that the role of impartial observer would be difficult to maintain; it would lead to ineffective observation. The centre of activity very soon becomes the table where the group is writing, planning and discussing. Only by going round, observing the groups, giving help where it is needed and generally participating in the activity is the observer going to gain any insight into the effectiveness of the learning process that the teacher has set in motion.

This is an appropriate stage at which to mention notetaking. It is possible that the senior management of the school will have devised some kind of schedule for classroom observation which has been negotiated with and agreed by the staff. It is also possible that the LEA will have designed some such instrument, though it is to be hoped that it would not seek to impose it on its schools. Although there is much experience in the United States of the use of schedules, there is no evidence that their detailed minutiae actually contribute to a clearer view of the classroom interactions. Counting blades of grass does not give the observer any concept of the field.

Nevertheless, an observer who goes into the classroom merely to receive impressions may well come out little wiser than when she went in. It is by no means necessary to attempt to cover every aspect of the teacher's performance in one visit and there is merit in negotiating with the teacher what in particular is being observed. A teacher may have doubts about the efficacy of his questioning techniques. Here there would be merit in the observer actually recording the wording of a range of questions and the kinds of response that they elicited, so that there could be discussion later on the extent to which open and closed questions had been used, and whether or not opportunities for stretching the pupils had been grasped. A teacher engaged in group work might welcome the close observation of the behaviour of a randomly chosen group in order that he may learn about their commitment to task, mutual support and attainment of goals.

If the observer is closely involved in the activities of the class, there will be no time for detailed notes. She needs to cultivate the habit of jotting down 'trigger' words which will act as reminders for the debriefing session which follows. Even if the lesson is one in which the observer adopts the 'fly on the wall' approach, were she to be seen by the class to be writing copiously throughout – as happens in a secondary school geography lesson on video (see Appendix 2) – she will almost certainly present herself to the pupils as assessor rather than appraiser. Comments like 'What mark did you get for the lesson, sir?' must therefore be expected.

Whatever the negotiated agreement, whether with the staff as a whole or with individuals as part of the preparation for observation, notetaking must be an open behaviour: the teacher must either have access to the notes if they are to be retained or be given an undertaking that they will be destroyed if they are used solely as the basis for a written report on the lesson, a copy of which the teacher must receive.

Agreeing the focus

Two at least of the pilot LEAs drew a valuable distinction between *general focus* and *specific focus* lesson observation. It is likely that the first observation will have a general focus so that the observer is able to view the learning process through a 'wide-angle lens'. Discussion of that lesson will then reveal areas upon which there might profitably be a specific focus during a later observation: whether pupils are effectively on task in a multi-activity groupwork lesson, for example. It is unrealistic to expect the observer to focus on more than two or three specific areas in one lesson. These should be areas agreeable to both the observer and the teacher; in practice there is unlikely to be any grounds for disagreement, since teachers rapidly accept that non-judgmental classroom observation helps them to improve their performance. They therefore readily suggest areas where observation will be of most benefit to them.

Contracting for debriefing

The teacher needs the assurance that time is being made available reasonably near to the lesson observation for a discussion on the outcomes. The observer needs to ensure that the occasion will be uninterrupted and that she will not be forced into concluding the discussion prematurely by the pressure of other activities. It is very difficult to anticipate just how long will be needed. It is irrelevant whether the lesson has appeared to the observer to be trouble free or to raise a multitude of issues: the teacher's needs do not necessarily equate with the observer's perceptions.

In planning for any debriefing one can only make an educated guess at the desirable duration. At the beginning of the debriefing session, it may be possible, while drawing up the agenda, to determine what will need immediate attention and will fit into the time that has been allowed and what can safely be held over until a further meeting can be arranged.

The contract must also include agreement on where the debriefing will take place. Our trialling of classroom observation has shown an overwhelming desire by primary teachers that it should take place on what

Figure 5.2 Debriefing

AFTER THE LESSON

- Confirm time and place for debriefing

- Give opportunity for self-evaluation

- Review aims and expectations

- Identify and analyse lesson strengths

- Identify and analyse lesson weaknesses

- Contract for further support

© Routledge 1991

they perceive to be home ground: their classroom. In secondary schools, presumably because there is a greater number of rooms that can be used for this purpose that do not have the connotations of the use of the headteacher's office, there is less strength of feeling about the location. Interestingly, teachers seem to regard privacy as less important than feeling at ease. This may be as well. However much one has sought to ensure that there will be no interruption, there will always be the occasion when a head will appear round the door and a voice call out: 'Oh, sorry! I didn't know you were busy!'

DEBRIEFING

It is possible, indeed very likely, that the teacher will want to begin to discuss the lesson immediately it is over, particularly in a secondary school where there may be a moment or two between the dismissal of one class and the arrival of the next. Except for some brief words of approbation or reassurance, it is better that nothing of substance is said until the debriefing meeting. Confirmation of the debriefing arrangements will often be a useful ploy for ensuring that a conversation which cannot be conveniently concluded is not begun.

Self-evaluation

One of the most important functions of classroom observation is to encourage self-awareness on the part of the teacher. It is therefore important that the debriefing begins with the teacher's own views on the merits and demerits of the lesson under review. It might be thought that the teacher will see only the good points of his lesson; but experience of this aspect of classroom observation indicates that this is rarely the case. Indeed, there is research evidence to show that self-evaluation is highly effective and that self-perceptions are generally accurate.

Even if this were not so, there would still be a strong argument for opening up a debriefing session by inviting the teacher to give his views. The greater likelihood in cases where self-evaluation is not accurate is that the teacher is excessively critical of his performance. In this situation the observer is in a position to moderate the self-criticism and, incidentally, place herself in the strong position of being the one who can say 'No, really, it was much better than you think'.

Nevertheless, there will be those who, whether or not they have perceived their own weaknesses, may be unwilling to disclose them to another. It is difficult for some teachers to rid themselves of the feeling that self-disclosure is in itself a weakness. We have detected at times an element of sexism: a man finding it difficult to admit to a woman colleague that he is less than perfect, professionally speaking! Situations like this may well call for the use of those influencing skills with which we deal in Chapter 8.

Classroom observation: self-evaluation

This is to help you to identify the strengths and weaknesses of the lesson that has just been observed.

Under each main heading there are examples of points you might consider. You may add to these if you wish.

How did you ensure that the pupils were readily able to get on with their work?

• Were materials prepared and available?

• Was the room suitably arranged?

• Were your instructions clear and well understood?

How did you encourage good standards of achievement?

• Did you relate well to all the children?

• Did you spend time with individuals/each group?

© Routledge 1991

- Was the task appropriate to the children's ability?

- Was the noise level acceptable and conducive to work?

How did you encourage an awareness of achievement?
- Did you conclude the lesson with a résumé or evaluation of what you had done?

- Was clearing up satisfactorily completed?

- Did the children enjoy the task?

- Did you enjoy the session?

What forward thinking have you established for the next lesson?

A probe may be needed to encourage the teacher into more open behaviour; occasionally it may even be necessary to 'unmask', where the teacher is in a state of self-deception.

A self-evaluation proforma can be helpful as a focus for the teacher's evaluation of his performance. We have used the one on pages 62–3 in our training for appraisal and it seems to have general application to most classroom situations and to primary and secondary schools alike. Some schools may well wish to construct their own. This is an exercise which, if done as a session of an in-service day, is valuable in its own right, since it promotes discussion on the criteria for good classroom performance. However, there is the danger of attempting to create a document which is all-inclusive and, in so doing, produce a white elephant because teachers will not have the time or the inclination to complete it. We have concentrated on three key areas of performance that relate approximately to the beginning, the middle and the end of the lesson. The questions have been phrased to promote an objective stance: phrasing such as 'Did you feel that . . .?', 'Did you think that . . .?' has been avoided.

It is also possible for the proforma to be used as an evaluation sheet by the observer. The purpose of its use in this way must be clearly understood by both the teacher and the observer: it is so that both parties can share perceptions of the way the lesson has gone. It is categorically not a document to be retained by the observer as an assessment of the lesson.

One of the merits of this procedure is that it becomes easy for both parties in the debriefing rapidly to identify those areas where they have the same perception and those where they differ. The explorations of the differences may well prove to be the more fruitful as the discussion continues.

It is unlikely that self-evaluation will ever be a discrete stage in the debriefing. Often it will lead naturally into the subsequent stages and then back from them again as the discussion progresses.

Aims and expectations

It may seem unnecessary that an item that has been dealt with at some length in the previous agenda now reappears; but the extent to which aims and expectations have or have not been met is a vital part of the debriefing. Teaching is, after all, a purposive activity and it is important that the main focus of discussion is on whether what has been achieved measures up to what were the intended outcomes. It is, however, important that neither party regards the aims as tablets of stone. Good lessons take account of the interests that the pupils bring into the classroom and, while the aim of the lesson should not be subverted, diversions on the way that take account of these interests are desirable and reflect the adaptive skills of the good teacher.

Strengths and weaknesses

The self-evaluation will already have identified some, at least, of these areas. The contribution of the observer is in part to offer an overview of the lesson since, whether participant or not, she has been better placed than the teacher to look at the structure of the lesson, the use of time, the effective use of teaching aids and so on; and in part to boost the self-confidence of the teacher. It follows therefore that the main concentration must be on strengths. Where weaknesses have been identified the observer must as far as possible be the enabler whereby these too can be translated into strengths.

There will of course be teachers who are teaching to the best of their ability but still not being very effective. If the content of their lessons is the problem, then it may be that they need in-service training to remedy deficiencies. If the methodology is at fault then they may be in need of sustained help from a departmental colleague or a curriculum coordinator. Since a key concern of the appraisal process is staff development, any indicators of areas where remediation is needed are clearly of value both to the individual teacher and to the school. In the past there have been two main impediments to making good deficiencies where these have been identified within the school. The first was that, when it was necessary for the headteacher to go to the LEA subject adviser in order to get such a teacher on an appropriate course, there was often a reluctance on the part of the teacher to have his weaknesses exposed − for so it would appear to him − to a representative of the authority. The second was that, even where there was agreement by the teacher, the LEA was in a situation of making judgments on competing needs for limited resources with what was frequently limited knowledge of the circumstances. The headteacher who was most persuasive − or most tenacious − would often win a place for her member of staff; and it could even happen that persuasion would be effective with one adviser and ineffective with another, regardless of the relative merits of the two cases.

The advent of the Grant Related In-Service Training funding, GRIST as it was first known, then LEATGS, and now GEST, changed the locus of much of the decision-making about in-service training from the advisory service to the schools. There was, in the early days, a wide range of practice by LEAs in the discretion they gave to schools, as a research study for the Manpower Services Commission of seven south-west LEAs revealed (Pilley and Poster, 1988). Since that survey was undertaken, schools have been increasingly empowered to evaluate for themselves competing needs for in-service training; and the introduction of local financial management in all secondary schools and many primary schools will consolidate that power.

In the updating and improvement of knowledge about curriculum content and of skills in pedagogic methodology, classroom observation has therefore an important part to play. The long-term career development in-service needs of each member of staff will, as will be seen in Chapter 7, be discussed either as an item on the agenda of or arising from the biennial appraisal interview, and of course will continue to be raised in career development interviews outside the appraisal process. Those more immediate needs that relate directly to classroom performance will arise most naturally from the observation process.

Contracting for further action

We have already indicated that the time set aside for debriefing may prove to be inadequate and that a further session may sometimes be needed. It is also possible that the observer and the teacher may find themselves at odds and both feel the need for the involvement of a third party; that serious differences have been observed between the curriculum as perceived by the teacher and that laid down by the school; that a lack of suitable resources or an absence of adequate support has been identified; that strategies for dealing with particular behavioural difficulties have not been satisfactorily thought through or communicated. We do not want to appear to be exaggerating the likelihood of any of these situations arising, but it is as well that senior managers in schools are aware of the possibility and of the time costs involved. In a number of cases when this has happened in schools where we have been responsible for appraisal training, headteachers have initially been alarmed at what seemed to them the unforeseen demands being made on the time of staff who were already heavily committed. Yet when we have discussed these cases individually, we have become aware that the situation disclosed through classroom observation would almost certainly have arisen in any event, and probably in terms that would have made even greater demands on staff time and nervous energy. Good school managers are increasingly alerted to the need to anticipate problem situations, having learnt that they seem invariably to arise when there is no time to deal with them. We hear a lot about crisis management these days, but effective crisis management is being able to manage one's affairs so that there are as few crises as possible!

The number of classroom observations for each teacher required of schools by the Secretary of State may prove to bear little relation to the actual needs of the school or the teacher. There will be many headteachers who will wish to find the time for the job to be done not according to the letter, but in the spirit of school improvement. The use of the word 'contract' is deliberate, implying a commitment to meet the needs of teachers for the benefit of the school and its pupils. Clearly staff, in planning their use of time, will have to evaluate one need against another before contracting; but contracts, once made, should be honoured if staff are to have confidence in the management of the school.

WHO WILL OBSERVE?

In over four years of working on appraisal with primary headteachers and senior staff we have observed a marked change in the response to this question. For some time there was a clear and almost universal expectation that, since the headteacher is responsible for the appraisal process, it must follow that the classroom observation, an integral part of that process, would also be her responsibility. The indication from the Interim Report of the pilot studies in appraisal (NDC, 1988) that the profession should be thinking in terms of an appraiser being responsible for no more than five appraisals caused some initial alarm; but for many this was quickly rationalised, except in the largest primary schools, into 'sharing the load with the deputy would be good for both of us' and 'I am sure we might manage six or seven each rather than involve someone else'. Yet even then there were primary headteachers who were urging their colleagues to consider appraisal not in isolation but as a feature in whole school development; and these were asking the vital question 'How can we give sufficient credibility to the role of the curriculum coordinators if we deprive them of an opportunity of observing their peers at work in the subject areas for which they are being given responsibility?' To create these opportunities within the framework of appraisal will not be easy; but to create it outside that framework will be far less easy, indeed, probably impossible to any worthwhile extent in the light of the time costs of appraisal itself.

We could not for one moment claim that this view is either widespread or even gathering considerable momentum; but at least it is being considered. Furthermore, those who are considering it are doing so in the recognition that it will inevitably impinge on the way many primary schools are currently run, demanding a more collegiate and open style of management. For some headteachers this surrender of autonomous power will not be easy; but there are many educationists (Dennison and Shenton, 1987; Wilkinson and Cave, 1988; Beare et al, 1989) who argue that there are considerable benefits in the greater managerial flexibility that obtains in the system of loose-coupling first propounded by Wieck (1976).

The very complexity of secondary schools, rather than any greater adherence to less hierarchical concepts of management theory, has led secondary headteachers with whom we have worked to be more immediately aware of the need to establish a devolved policy for classroom observation. Yet, in considering to whom to devolve, interesting issues of policy arise. Some of these are indeed concerned with existing managerial structures and style. There are schools whose appraisal teams have been clearly selected from the most senior staff and one consequence of this has been that major departments may well be represented on the team and minor ones may well not. This then raises the cognate question of the credibility as observers of classroom performance of those who are not specialists in a given subject.

Two clearly irreconcilable arguments are raised: that at secondary level familiarity with subject content is of crucial importance; and that the classroom observer is concerned with generic teaching abilities and not with content. Common sense suggests that extreme situations are not tenable: for example, that a teacher, however senior, whose knowledge of science extends no further than the content of the O level examination in general science twenty years ago will have credibility as observer of a fifth year lesson in physics today. There are three possible solutions worthy of consideration. The first is that one criterion for the selection of the team which undergoes appraisal training is that it has, collectively, credibility over the range of level and subject within the school. Within this solution there is the expectation that classroom observation and appraisal interview will be conducted by the same member of staff. The second is that classroom observation is not necessarily conducted by members of the team that has had full appraisal training, although plainly some training will be required. Within any department, therefore, one or more members will be responsible for classroom observation; and the outcomes of that observation will be passed on to the appraiser as part of the data collection. Since the views of a departmental head are likely to be sought by appraisers during the data collection over a range of non-class contact responsibilities of the members of his staff – contribution to departmental staff meetings or to the creation and maintenance of resources, for example – the classroom observation will thus be placed in the context of the total contribution to the department. The third – and this applies in the main to schools where there is already a climate of team teaching, shared planning, easy access to or exchange with colleagues' classes – is that of peer appraisal for the classroom observation element.

WHO IS BEING OBSERVED?

Initially this question may puzzle some readers; indeed, there will be many to whom it is self-evident that only by observing the learning process rather than the teaching process is it possible to find out whether or not a lesson is effective. Even when the teacher is centre-stage, setting tasks or conducting a plenary discussion, the observer's key role is to study the reactions of individual members of the class. It is unlikely that in any class there will be full attention throughout the lesson from every student; or that there will be full comprehension of every issue. The observer plays a valuable role in weighing the contributions of the class in answering, questioning, listening, performing tasks, helping each other in an appropriate manner, and so on, against some admittedly subjective standard she has in mind. That standard cannot be prescribed. A teacher may perform outstandingly well with a difficult class, even though the performance levels are significantly inferior to those of another class. This is why performance criteria, though they may appear to be valuable in establishing common ground among schools, are counterproductive unless they are moderated by the circumstances that prevail in the class or the school. This is why it is important that the observer comes in fully briefed about likely discordant or antisocial behaviours that will affect the outcomes of the lesson. It is also why the observer's eyes should be predominantly on the students rather than on the teacher.

TRAINING FOR CLASSROOM OBSERVATION

There are three key elements to training for classroom observation and, in our experience, one full day of training for appraisal needs to be spent on these for both appraisers and appraisees. If this is to be a whole staff activity, then it needs to take place on an in-service day. It needs a team of tutors – one for every six to eight members of staff – who have planned the day and themselves trialled the materials that follow.

Criteria for good classroom performance

This activity is best promoted through a brainstorming session. It gives rise to useful group discussion and highlights, through the different value sets that become apparent, the importance of consensus within a school.

Although brainstorming is now a widely used technique in in-service training, we have always found it helpful to remind workshop members of the 'rules':

- all ideas are equally good and should be put up on the flipchart without discussion or comment;
- the scribe has equal rights with other members of the group to make contributions;
- a hiatus in contributions should not be taken to mean that ideas have been exhausted – often the best contributions come after a lull;
- reaching the end of a flipchart sheet is not an indication that no further contributions are called for!

The encouragement to all to contribute, without regard to status, is certainly the most important initial benefit of brainstorming. However, the sheer profusion of what is now on the flipchart may lead to confusion if nothing further is done after the generation of ideas. What is more, the opportunity must be given for the reconciliation of any differences of opinion within the group. This is best done by requiring a second stage activity.

Groups are now invited to create generic categories for the ideas on the flipchart and to recast those ideas under these main headings. One such heading might well be classroom atmosphere; another, teacher–pupil relationships; yet another, classroom organisation. It will often happen that an idea will be seen to be relevant to more than one category. This is in itself valuable in that it demonstrates the holistic nature of criteria.

Whether or not there is value in a reporting back session is a matter for the workshop tutor to decide. In general we have found that there is as much benefit – and a considerable saving of valuable training time – if the final flipcharts are displayed for groups to view in their own time, possibly in a coffee break, before a plenary session. This avoids the syndrome of the rapporteur of the fifth group to be called upon saying 'Well, I've nothing much to add on behalf of my group, but . . .' and then speaking for the allotted three minutes anyway, lest he gives the impression that his group has not worked as well as the previous groups! What is far more valuable in a plenary session than a tedious reporting back is for the tutor to have spent a little preparation time drawing from the flipchart display some general conclusions and discussion points.

The training module on page 71 offers three variants for the activity. We have found that looking at the task from three perspectives is illuminating and promotes useful discussion.

Training for observation briefing

The elements of the briefing process described in Chapter 5 (see Figure 5.1, page 53) serve as a useful introduction to the next phase, which requires about 45 minutes in all. There are two possible approaches after the introduction. The first requires role play by two tutors, one as observer, the other as teacher of the lesson being observed. Working either from a written lesson preparation – the English lesson plan on page 56 can be used in secondary schools since it links with the narrative of the lesson which follows on pages 75–6 – or through verbal communication, the tutors improvise the briefing process. Discussion then takes place in groups or in plenary about the effectiveness of what the workshop members have seen.

Alternatively, a video of a briefing session, such as that between the Head of the Infants Department and the Deputy Head of the Somerset school (see Appendix 2), can be played and similarly discussed, in preparation for viewing the video of the lesson which follows.

Training for classroom observation

There are two possible sources of material for training in classroom observation: video and case study. Although videos of classroom situations have their advocates we have some reservations about this strategy for a number of reasons. First, except for very young children or in situations where there is a very high level of pupil activity, as, for example, dance,

Classroom performance criteria

For a lesson to be observed with real benefit to the teacher, it is vital that there is agreement on what constitutes good classroom practice.

Appoint a scribe and for 30 minutes brainstorm the question assigned to your group:

GROUP 1: By what criteria do you judge effective teaching?

GROUP 2: What are the conditions under which pupils learn best?

GROUP 3: What makes a good teacher?

If there are more than three groups, Group 4 also undertakes the assignment of Group 1 and so on.

Keep to the following rules while you brainstorm:

- At this stage all ideas are equally valuable. Do not debate them yet.

- Do not ask for explanations or elucidation yet.

- Give everyone the opportunity to contribute, including your scribe.

- Do not worry if there is a brief silence. More ideas may be forthcoming in a moment or two.

After 15–20 minutes, bring this part of the brainstorming to a conclusion. Now look at the ideas and identify some common headings under which you can group the contributions. Do not worry if some ideas seem to belong to more than one heading. Set out those generalised headings on a fresh flipchart as your responses to the question you have been addressing. Give yourselves what remains of the 30 minutes for this second activity.

drama or some areas of CDT, most pupils are decidedly conscious of the presence of the camera and react accordingly. In the USA this appears not to be the case. Video is widely used in initial and in-service teacher training and by serving teachers wishing to evaluate their own classroom performance. However, we would do well to borrow from other cultures only when our situations are similar; and we have not yet reached the degree of sophistication with television technology that they have across the Atlantic.

Secondly, a choice must be made between the fixed camera and the camera operated by a colleague or a technician. The fixed camera is less obtrusive but has the disadvantages that it invariably focuses on the teacher, that it requires the teacher to be static and that it cannot take cognisance of pupil reaction, except indirectly as we observe the teacher's response to incidents which we have not witnessed but which we may have been able to deduce. The hand-held camera is able to move readily from teacher to learner, but has two main disadvantages: it is far more visible to the class and consequently intervenes in the learning process; and the operator, who may or may not have pedagogic skills, effectively edits the video by what he decides to have in frame at any given time.

Thirdly, even where good video material can be found, the training time cost is too great if those in training are required to view a full lesson before any discussion can take place on the training experience. With skilful editing it may be possible to reduce the running time to 15–20 minutes, but even then there is the danger of over-concentration on the teacher-centred activities that open and close most lessons at the expense of the pupil-centred activities that may be most rewarding in real classroom observation.

Finally, if they are to be of real value in a training experience, videos must be well edited, both technically and from the point of view of the trainer, and professionally produced. Recently we have been pleased to find, having previously viewed with increasing frustration a number of amateur attempts, several highly professional productions now on the market which we feel we can recommend (see Appendix 2). Some classroom observations are already edited down to manageable time. Others run the full length of a lesson and would need to be trimmed to suit the needs of the trainer and the time available.

Written case studies, however, have the merit that they can be so structured that they bring out the salient points that the trainer desires, in particular those that are felt to be of especial relevance to that school or LEA. They should, it must be said, be drawn from real situations, though obviously there may be some modification of the detail or condensing of several experiences. There is a temptation – which all good trainers must school themselves to resist – to over-dramatise or even sensationalise situations. The closer the simulation is to reality the more effective it will be as training material.

For a school conducting its own in-service sessions in classroom observation, it is possible to create a case study by observing the lesson of a willing volunteer and then writing it up. It may be, however, that those who are prepared to volunteer will be teachers of such confidence that there is not very much to learn from the case study. It is not that one wants bad lessons for case studies – far from it – but rather that there must be situations within the lesson that will promote discussion within the group or the plenary.

The secondary school case study on pages 75–6 follows directly from the lesson plan on page 56. For the primary case study on pages 78–80, trainers may invite groups to recreate the lesson notes from the text of the lesson before issuing the instructions for the training module on page 81; alternatively, and particularly if time is at a premium, they may tell their workshop members to assume the existence of an appropriate lesson plan. For the early years case study on pages 82–4 the lesson plan is contained within the materials presented.

In each case the case study is presented to groups for discussion with two main intentions: that they should test out their criteria for effective classroom performance against it; and that they should plan how they will conduct the debriefing session that follows the lesson. Trainers may well find that groups which appeared to be of one mind over the criteria will now become quite disputatious over their interpretations of the merits and demerits of the lesson itself; and, further, in spite of having accepted the importance of building on the teacher's strengths, immediately identify a succession of weaknesses in the lesson.

One training strategy is to issue the self-evaluation proforma on pages 62–3 to the group members and to invite them to complete it rapidly, half of them from the perspective of the teacher and half from that of the observer. This enlivens discussion, since those taking the role of the teacher may well be very defensive of incidents which those in the observer role may be equally quick to condemn.

However useful the discussion on the lesson itself may be, what matters most is that the group gives time to consideration of what, as observers, they judge to be the most important points to bring up in the debriefing session that follows and how they propose to introduce them. Following group work, there are four possibilities for the next session:

- in plenary session one group – and the choice of which group is best determined by a tutor going around during the latter part of the discussion and identifying one whose views will promote constructive controversy – presents its proposals for general discussion by the workshop members;
- two tutors again role-play the observer and teacher, now in the debriefing session, and groups are then invited to say how they would have handled the situation differently;

- from one of the groups a volunteer is found to play the role of the observer while a tutor role-plays the teacher;
- within each group, one member of the observer subgroup and one of the teacher subgroup role-play the debriefing.

The last is in many ways the most effective, since it achieves the active involvement of more workshop members. It works best, however, when there is a tutor available to guide each group. We use this for the instructions which accompany each of the case studies which follow; but trainers will of course substitute whatever instructions best suit their circumstances. Needless to say, the overriding aim of the session is to establish that the needs of the teacher are paramount, provided that they lie within the parameters of the whole school policy.

CONCLUSION

If training for appraisal is to be experiential, as we believe it must be for both appraisers and appraisees, there should now be some time available between this training phase and the one which follows. Three to four weeks will provide the opportunity for some members of staff, at least, to engage experientially in classroom observation. What they discover will make a valuable discussion session at the opening of the next training phase, to reinforce skills and confidence, and equally to identify areas of misconception and disagreement.

Classroom observation: secondary

The introduction to the lesson goes well. The children are aware of the presence of the observer, but are not particularly concerned. If anything, they are making an extra effort to be attentive and to answer the teacher's questions. They are quite taken with the OHP (which deals with a supposed event concerning an imaginary pop group) and they quickly identify, without actually being asked, similar tendentious headlines that they have observed in the papers. In fact, this part of the lesson could have continued much longer but the teacher draws the introduction to an end after just over ten minutes.

The teacher now picks up one sheaf of photocopies of newspaper articles and says: 'I expect that your family is like mine. We have one daily newspaper regularly. Sometimes we see a second paper, usually when my husband goes to London on business and has to catch an early train. But I don't suppose anyone here sees as many as six different papers.'

A hand goes up. 'I do, Miss.' There's a gasp of disbelief. Then someone laughs. 'Course he does! He's got a newspaper round!'

The teacher joins in the laughter. 'I had better be careful with my choice of words. Does anyone *read* six newspapers?' There are no takers.

The teacher draws from the class the fact that newspapers present the same story in different styles and they readily accept the idea of spending a short time looking at the treatment of one story in six different newspapers. She concludes: 'I would like you to tell me next week if you think this has helped you with the articles you are going to write.' There is a buzz of interest and one child calls out: 'What articles, Miss? Tell us about it now please!' and another: 'For a *real* newspaper?' There is laughter, which she allows, but she is firm that she will tell them about it at the proper time and the questioning subsides. She tells them what they are to look for in the newspaper articles that they now have in front of them and she tells the group leaders that they are in charge of their group work once the individual reading has been completed.

There are some problems here. Some bright children have seized on short articles while some slow readers have ended up with longer articles with a higher level of vocabulary. Although she has deliberately provided one more newspaper cutting than there are members of any group, changing over articles does not work very smoothly. After five minutes she tells them it is time to start answering the questions on the cyclostyled sheet and she repeats that the group leaders are in charge of their groups.

The noise level rises as the groups begin to try to answer the questions, but stays within what the observer regards as acceptable limits, though the teacher casts one or two anxious glances in her direction. The observer gives a reassuring smile. The teacher now goes from one group to another, either when the group leader signals that she is wanted or when she thinks fit. Suddenly there is a cry from a member of Group 6, who says: 'Miss, my group leader won't help me! I don't understand all the words!' A voice says: 'Learn to read, you dummy!' Laughter. The teacher hushes the disruption and goes herself to help.

After fifteen minutes few groups have done more than complete the first two tasks and embarked upon the third. There are anxious cries of 'How much longer have we got, Miss?' and it is clear that they need the time she has allotted for the plenary session if they are all to have completed even the third task. She tells them that she has decided that they can spend until the end of the lesson and that she will ask them to talk about what they have found out in the next lesson. Someone says: 'What about those articles we are going to write then, Miss?' She replies that they will still be doing that task and they appear to be satisfied.

Two minutes from the end she asks the group leaders to collect the newspaper articles and bring them to her. This they do although it takes rather more than two minutes. Fortunately it is lunch time and this class is not in the first sitting.

After the children have gone the teacher says to the observer: 'It's no good. I just don't seem to be able to manage time properly.'

TRAINING MODULE (ONE HOUR)

Work in two subgroups, one considering this lesson from the point of view of the teacher, the other that of the observer. In the light of the criteria you have earlier established, identify the main strengths and weaknesses of the lesson.

The teacher subgroup completes the self-evaluation proforma. The observer subgroup plans the agenda for the debriefing, deciding particularly what it is best to highlight to achieve improved teaching performance.

One member of each subgroup then volunteers to role-play the teacher and the observer in the debriefing.

Classroom observation: primary

BACKGROUND

The Juniper Street Primary School is sited in an urban area where, because of recent housing association reclamation of residential accommodation that had fallen into a state of disrepair, the number on roll has risen significantly. The school is a mixture of turn-of-the-century and postwar buildings and is well maintained. There are several attractive displays in corridors and classrooms, including the one that the headteacher is about to visit, but not consistently throughout the school. The headteacher, newly appointed, is seeking to widen the staff approach – mainly chalk and talk – to something less formal.

The teacher of this class is a mature entrant to the profession now in her third year of teaching but her first in this school. The class is second-year junior, mixed ability, twenty-seven on roll. There are six children from ethnic minorities, four Pakistani, all girls, and two Afro-Caribbean, both boys. The children are naturally boisterous but generally cooperative. There is, however, one boy who can be very disruptive and who has already been referred to the LEA's psychologist. He will often attack other children or their work for no apparent reason.

It is midway through the spring term and this is the headteacher's first full-scale observation though she has of course dropped in from time to time the previous term.

THE LESSON

The teacher is in the classroom waiting for the children to come in from morning play. She has ready a wide range of fruits and vegetables cut up into quarters or slices, drawing paper, paint, palettes, water pots. She has just fetched a tray of lenses and microscopes from the school science store.

As they enter the room the children notice the fruit and start asking: 'Miss, what we gonna do?' The teacher claps her hands for silence and tells the children to sit down quietly or they will not find out. Freddie arrives late and the teacher waits until he is seated and attentive.

'This is a lesson on observation. This morning we are going to look really closely at various fruits and vegetables. First you will use your eyes and then you will look at them through the lens or microscope. Then I want one in each pair to paint or draw what can be seen with the naked eye and the other the enlargement that is seen through the magnifier. You will have to be very observant to get the right detail. The Head has come to see how well you do and I shall ask her at the end of the lesson to select the best work for display.'

First she shows the various fruits and checks that the children know the names of them all. At one stage an Asian girl says something in Punjabi which causes her friends to giggle. [The teacher has in fact mispronounced the name of an Asian vegetable.] Several members of the class hush them, saying 'She won't let us start if you talk'. The teacher concludes her introduction and distributes the specimens.

The pairs start to compare their specimen with those of their neighbours and the noise level rises. The teacher calls for silence: 'I have not yet told you exactly what I want you to do, have I? I will not continue until you are quite quiet.' The children put down their specimens, face the front and settle down. The teacher waits for a few laggards.

'Now what do you think you might look for?'

Replies come thick and fast: colour, texture, blemishes, seed configurations, irregularity of shape and so on, though not in these words. The teacher writes down a number of key words and asks a few further questions. Someone asks: 'Can we taste them, Miss?' and there is laughter. The teacher replies: 'I don't think you would like a raw potato, would you? After the lesson I will let anyone who wants taste one or two fruits that you may not have seen before. But do touch them. That will help you to draw them.'

Several children take up their pencils. 'No, don't start yet. Spend some time looking. Compare what you see with your eye with what you can see through the magnifier.' They get to work and do as they have been told. The noise level is high but not unduly so. She goes from pair to pair.

Suddenly there is a wail. 'Miss, Freddie's not letting me look! Why do I have to have him for a partner?' Freddie just grins and shows no sign of sharing. The teacher takes Freddie by the hand to another desk and gives him a magnifier and a piece of turnip. She stands by him for a few minutes.

After a while she tells them to stop and put down their magnifiers. There is a delay while two pairs carry on discussing what they have seen. She repeats her instruction. She then selects several children to describe what they have seen, prompting them with various questions like 'Was it smooth? Did it glisten? Did the marks remind you of anything?'

Next she explains that it is time to draw and paint. 'Remember, we want detail, so you may need fine brushes for some of the painting. Don't forget what we did a few weeks ago when we looked at the colour spectrum and experimented with mixing colours.' She tells them how long they have until lunch time and once again goes from desk to desk, encouraging and helping, asking questions frequently.

Freddie starts to flick paint and there are cries of 'Miss! Miss!' She takes away his paints, tells him off and gives him some crayon colouring that he had started the previous day. She sits him near her desk. She now lets the pairs work on their own unless she is called.

Three minutes before the end of the lesson she tells everyone to stop, organises the storage of finished and unfinished work and delegates the clearing up to two girls who volunteer. Several ask to try one of the exotic fruits and make faces at the unusual taste.

TRAINING MODULE (ONE HOUR)

Work in two subgroups, one considering this lesson from the point of view of the teacher, the other that of the observer. In the light of the criteria you have earlier established, identify the main strengths and weaknesses of the lesson.

The teacher subgroup completes the self-evaluation proforma. The observer subgroup plans the agenda for the debriefing, deciding particularly what it is best to highlight to achieve improved teaching performance.

One member of each subgroup then volunteers to role-play the teacher and the observer in the debriefing.

Classroom observation: early years

BACKGROUND

Willow Infants School is a two-form entry school in a socially and ethnically mixed area on the city outskirts. The headteacher and her staff are firmly committed to realising the National Curriculum and the parents for the most part are appreciative of their efforts, being strongly achievement-orientated.

We are observing a class of thirty-two first-year infants, all of whom have passed their fifth birthday and have had at least one term of pre-schooling. The teacher has a General Assistant, Mrs Brown, but, owing to economies, there is no Welfare Assistant, though there is in the class a multiply-handicapped child, spastic and with two hearing aids.

LESSON PLAN

In the briefing meeting the teacher has shared with the observer her aims and expectations. The lesson centres on writing and writing-related activities. The children are in groups but writing is taught on an individual basis. Each child has a specific task and, once that task is satisfactorily completed, chooses the next activity. At 10.30 a.m. they will go to a first year assembly before going out to play, but otherwise the session is continuous. It begins with the children all together with the teacher planning the work they will do, and ends with them all together again telling or showing what they have done.

The groups are as follows:
- Group 1: in the writing corner at a table within easy reach of word-banks, etc. They will begin by drawing a picture of the lesson theme and then write the 'story'.
- Group 2: with Mrs Brown at the science table where they will observe shell patterns and draw shapes and spirals.
- Group 3: at painting easels near to the science table where Mrs Brown can supervise them.
- Group 4: on the carpet area with construction toys. Their task is to make something 'that can fly'. Derek, the handi-capped child, is with this group and has a bucket of Duplo.
- Group 5: has pencils, paper, scissors and shapes of garden creatures. They are to make cut-outs to fix on a pre-pared picture of a garden.

© Routledge 1991

All these activities relate to hand/eye coordination and control and are a preparation for writing.

In addition there is a table with jigsaw and shape-matching puzzles and a listening table equipped with tape recorders and story tapes.

THE LESSON

At 9 a.m. the observer arrives to see the whole class sitting on a central carpet area. After registration the teacher encourages the children to talk about last night's event: a family Bonfire Night party in the school grounds to which most of the children came, bringing their parents. The children are very excited and all want to talk at once, but the teacher is firm about taking turns. After ten minutes she changes the subject and shows them some snails in a box with grass and earth. She explains how the morning rain makes them active, demonstrating with the aid of a small watering can. There are also snails in smaller boxes with magnifying lids which she passes round for the children to look at more closely. Then she settles the children in their groups.

For a while everyone is quiet and busy. The teacher is helping Gary in Group 1 to write 'This is me'. She gives him the words to copy. At this point a quarrel breaks out in the carpet area and the teacher goes to mediate. She prompts the children to explain what they are doing and asks Derek to tell her about his Duplo. He has managed to fit three pieces together. She does not understand what he says but the other children explain.

Group 2 have tired of drawing and are eager to paint. With difficulty, Mrs Brown persuades Groups 2 and 3 to change places. Two children go to the listening table and everyone settles down again.

In Group 1 Jennifer has started to write using the word-bank independently, and the teacher sees that she needs to add more words. Scott has also gone ahead without help, but it is pretend writing. He tells the teacher what he thinks he has written and the teacher gives him a version to copy.

Group 5 are having problems cutting out shapes. The observer sits with them and helps.

A few minutes later two children from the science table decide to help their friend Derek. He does not want to be helped and flies into a screaming tantrum. The teacher picks him up to comfort him and, when he calms down, tells Mrs Brown to take him into the book corner and read him a story. The class is disturbed and the teacher spends a few minutes making sure that all are again usefully occupied.

Darren, who has finished making an aeroplane, has gone to the science table and calls out that a snail has escaped. Mrs Brown is still with Derek so the teacher goes to return the snail to the box, but the lid is missing. She puts the snail in the large box and then notices that, unobserved at the listening table, two little girls are unwinding a tape. One of them is looking at it through the magnifying lid. The teacher restores the lid, takes the tape away and sends the girls to tidy the Home Corner.

The teacher continues to work with the children at the writing table for another ten minutes but by then there is a good deal of aimless moving from place to place. She leaves the writing table, claps her hands and says 'I am going to listen to the writing group. While I do that I want everyone else to tidy their corners very quietly. When everything is tidy come and sit on the carpet and you can show us all the things you have been making.' When they are all sitting on the carpet she chooses three to show what they have been making. There are cries of 'Please, Miss! It's my turn, Miss!' The teacher says, 'No, we have to stop now for assembly. Does anybody want to go to the toilet?' Mrs Brown goes with the children to supervise.

As the children file into assembly, the teacher says: 'Mrs Brown, could I have a word with you at lunchtime?'

TRAINING MODULE (ONE HOUR)

Work in two subgroups, one considering this lesson from the point of view of the teacher, the other that of the observer. In the light of the criteria you have earlier established, identify the main strengths and weaknesses of the lesson.

The teacher subgroup completes the self-evaluation proforma. The observer subgroup plans the agenda for the debriefing, deciding particularly what it is best to highlight to achieve improved teaching performance.

One member of each subgroup then volunteers to role-play the teacher and the observer in the debriefing.

Chapter 6

Goalsetting

It may seem that appraisal is introducing the teaching profession to a whole new vocabulary, and goalsetting is one of those words to which some teachers may initially respond adversely. Yet there is no need for feelings of concern. Teachers have always set themselves goals: in the classroom, learning attainments for their pupils; in management, in relation to those for whom they are responsible; for themselves, in improving their skills.

We have ourselves a very strong preference for the use of the word *goal* rather than *target*, and we find this view widely shared by teachers with whom as trainers we have been engaged. This is not mere idiosyncrasy. Targets in the context of the workplace, whether that is school or factory, tend to imply that which is quantifiable, in terms either of output or of the time taken to achieve the desired end. We regret the growing use of this word in connection with appraisal, in the report of the National Steering Group, for example, and in some books and articles on appraisal training. In this book we intend to hold to the use of those words which, while not lacking precision, nevertheless reflect the greater flexibility that is desirable in teacher appraisal.

When schools and LEAs first turned their attention to training for appraisal, there was a tendency to focus on the appraisal interview as the key element of the process and to give less thought to the stages and events which had led up to it. Just as managers in any enterprise need to know the aims and objectives of an innovative activity before they can evaluate its success, so we in schools need to agree the goals for and with teaching staff long before any appraisal can take place.

It is as well also to clarify other terminology that will be used in this chapter: immediately, *job description* and *job specification*.

JOB DESCRIPTION

Most readers will at some time or other have seen job descriptions for teaching posts, many of them, unfortunately, poorly devised. Some are excessively complex, introducing elements relating to conditions of service or details about the school, the LEA, the neighbourhood, the governing body and so on. It is not that applicants will have no interest in these facts; indeed, most of them should be part of the school's routine hand-out to any enquirer. It is rather that the job description should be self-standing, dealing solely with the areas of responsibility for which a candidate is being sought.

Some appear to be primarily concerned with asking for qualities like enthusiasm, imagination, good communication skills and the like. It is difficult to conceive of many situations in which an intending applicant says to himself: 'Oh dear, so they want enthusiasm for this post, do they? I think I had better not proceed with my application'. Certainly these qualities will be expected in applicants. Questions about them are better directed to those offering references or looked for in the candidates' letters of application.

The job description on page 88 comes from a school that believes in plain and precise language and in clarity of intention. It is offered for two reasons: to illustrate that a job description will often be phrased in such a way as to allow for some flexibility; and to enable teachers, particularly in school-based training situations, to look at the way the key responsibilities listed here compare with those in a comparable post in their own school or appear in advertisements in the educational press. With a few changes of wording, this job description would be equally applicable to the post of deputy in a primary school of reasonable size.

JOB SPECIFICATION

There was a time, little more than a decade ago, when *role definition* was the phrase increasingly being used in schools to define the apportionment of responsibilities and the delineation of professional relationships (Poster, 1976). Today we are more likely to encounter the term *job specification*. What matters is not the term used but what we understand by it. It is possible that, in preferring *role*, teachers were subconsciously seeking to distance themselves from those who had *jobs*. Teaching was, it might be argued, a profession comparable with that of the doctor, the lawyer, a comparability that, unfortunately, did not extend to the salaries teachers were paid.

Job, then, let it be; and let us focus above all on the need for it to be specified. The reasons for this have less to do with appraisal than with good management. A job specification for each member of staff is essential if there is to be clarity about what people are responsible for and to whom they are responsible. Furthermore, they need to know to whom and how to refer when they reach the boundaries of their own decision-making role.

A job specification must not be confused with a job description. The latter relates solely to the post, not the incumbent, and indicates what the

Job description

APPOINTMENT OF DEPUTY HEAD: SECONDARY

The postholder will join the senior management team and will share in the overall management of the school. Whilst the major responsibilities will relate to student affairs, the precise job specification will take account of the particular strengths, experience and interests of the successful candidate.

KEY RESPONSIBILITIES

- Management of the pastoral system through year heads and tutors.

- Ensuring that the curriculum and its delivery are appropriate to all students.

- Monitoring of students' personal development, academic progress, behaviour and performance.

- Ensuring effective communication and consultation between the school, parents and students.

- Transfer arrangements with the neighbourhood primary schools.

- Liaison with external support, welfare and social agencies.

- Oversight of reporting procedures and the continuing development of the Record of Achievement.

- School disciplinary procedures.

© Routledge 1991

governors and the headteacher are seeking when a vacancy arises. When an appointment is made there are often significant differences between what has been sought and what has been obtained. Sometimes appointments are made where the successful candidate lacks certain of the requirements but has other attributes of which the school can make good use; and in such cases a school may well have on the staff a member of staff whose job specification can be modified to compensate for this candidate's deficiencies. Sometimes – and particularly in these days of severe teacher shortages in many areas of the country – a school will appoint a 'best fit' candidate rather than leave a post entirely vacant. The job specification must always reflect what the postholder is actually required and competent to do and not be a pious hope incapable of realisation. The job specification leads to goalsetting, and goalsetting in its turn sets up the criteria whereby the teacher will be appraised. It follows, therefore, that the selection of realistic and realisable goals is vital to the success of the appraisal process.

GOALSETTING

Figure 6.1 outlines the key considerations in goalsetting. There are, it will be seen, three elements to the job specification without which goalsetting would be a difficult, if not an impossible exercise: the job purpose, the key result areas and activities.

The first of these is self-explanatory: we can only begin to define the goals of any job if we have a clear and unequivocal statement of what that job is. However, the job purpose gives no indication of what will be needed to meet the requirements of the job; and the next step is therefore to identify its possible component areas. They are *key* because they are vital to the success of the job; and they are *result* areas because what the teacher accomplishes in these areas will demonstrate that success.

What the teacher sets out to achieve in any key result area will, however, depend on what *activities* he undertakes. Activities are not synonymous with objectives: an activity may have a number of objectives. It is better to think of activities as a sub-set of a particular key result area, breaking down one broad field of the job into its relevant constituent parts.

All three elements of the job specification, and their relationship with goalsetting, will be dealt with at greater length in the following pages.

It is important at this stage to observe that a number of LEAs produce blueprint 'specifications', which are in fact entirely concerned with contractual obligations. Though there may well be many teachers who regret the circumstances which have brought about this state of affairs, preferring the happier pre-contract days when teachers did the job without being required to account for the hours, such a document is nevertheless required, as a safeguard for both employer and employee. However, this specification has more to do with conditions of service than with the

Figure 6.1 Goalsetting

Goalsetting requires that there be a precise *job specification*. A job specification consists of:

- the job purpose
- key result areas
- activities associated with each KRA

The JOB PURPOSE states what the job exists for and is expressed in terms which point to future results: 'in order to . . .', for example. The statement of purpose should be *unique* to that post.

The key result areas are groupings of activities in which it is *essential* to achieve results in order to satisfy the job purpose. They must also be areas important enough to be appraised. There is no set figure for how many KRAs there should be for any one job specification; three is generally the minimum, six the maximum.

Activities describe the means of achieving each KRA in the job purpose. Activities tend to be either *innovative* or *maintenance* in character. The latter are no less important than the former.

From the three elements – job purpose, KRAs and activities – the headteacher [or his/her delegated representative] and the member of staff jointly establish the GOALS of the appraisee. Goals indicate agreed expectations of achievement or attainment, if possible within an agreed period of time. Longer-term goals may need to be broken down into phases.

Goals are:
GENERIC: applicable to all teachers holding that particular post or type of post; or
SPECIFIC: relevant to the particular needs of the school or skills of that teacher.

Goals need to be related to a school's overall DEVELOPMENT PLAN.

specific job within the school; and governors and headteachers would do well to keep them well apart, both conceptually and physically. A job specification, unlike the conditions of service, is a document which is the basis of negotiation between individuals and the institution in order to bring about the most effective deployment of the teaching force, both for the professional development of the teachers and, needless to say, for the benefit of the students.

The job purpose

A job purpose is a statement defining in broad terms that for which the postholder is held accountable. It might well be thought that the purpose of a teaching job is self-evident, almost certainly implicit in the title of the post – language curriculum coordinator, for example, or staff development coordinator – and in any case clearly understood at the time of the appointment. Yet time can blur the memory, headteachers may come and go, new governors will be appointed. An accurately phrased job purpose is a safeguard for all concerned.

There are two important matters which merit elaboration. It is not pedantic to require that the job purpose points to future outcomes. Generalised statements like 'to organise the department' mean very little and are open to misconstruction. The form of words used should be descriptive of the *end results* for which the job holder is held accountable.

The second point concerns the reference to the uniqueness of the job purpose to a particular post. There can, of course, be two or more main professional grade teachers of a subject for whom the same job purpose is appropriate. All that is required for this to be true is that their jobs are interchangeable. It is the post which is unique, not the postholder. In practice very few, if any, teachers have job specifications which are not unique to them: while the main teaching role may be the same as that of another teacher, there is nearly always some aspect or extension of the role which is person-specific.

Key result areas

Every assistant teacher in the school will have two key result areas which are immediately identifiable: in teaching and in caring. Additionally, now that schools have become such complex and demanding institutions, most teachers will have a managerial role of some kind, regardless of whether it attracts an incentive allowance. For some, the more senior staff, this managerial key result area may be of prime importance to the smooth running of the school; but, however important, it will never wholly supersede the personal teaching and caring role. It may, however, lead to curriculum KRAs seemingly appearing twice, once because the postholder has responsibilities as a teacher and on the other occasion because she has responsibilities as manager. This apparent duplication is proper, but it is possible to avoid confusion by discriminating clearly between teaching and managerial KRAs. Figure 6.2 lists the general range of KRAs to be found in any school. Needless to say, the nomenclature is not of crucial importance. Some schools may well prefer learning to teaching, or community to outreach. Alternatively, they may have other classifications to add which are important to them and reflect their organisational experience.

Key result areas will normally alter only as a result of a modification in the job purpose or, of course, when there is a significant change in the job itself. It does happen sometimes, however, that the management style of a school has built into it a rotation of key result areas. One secondary school, for example, with a five faculty curriculum structure, allocates to each member of the senior management team responsibility for liaison with a faculty, but rotates that faculty year by year. In some primary schools the headteacher and the deputy interchange one key result area from time to time, partly for revitalisation, but particularly to give the deputy the widest possible experience in preparation for a future headship. At a time when, in spite of early retirement, there is a block on promotion prospects for many in mid-career, job change is becoming increasingly popular. When a complete job change – which would require a new job description and specification – is impossible or undesirable, a job shift involving the internal exchange of a key result area is often a very satisfying alternative.

Normally, however, key result areas will remain unchanged. What may change, though, is their relative importance. This may be a consequence of school policy: the close relationship between the school's development plan and individual goals will be referred to later. Sometimes it is simply a matter of having achieved desired goals in one KRA and of having only maintenance activities to take their place. Consequently, the opportunity now exists to raise for the time being the status of another KRA.

Activities

A KRA actually does no more than delineate an area of responsibility. It does nothing to detail how that responsibility will be met. This is the function of *activities*. These are the means of giving substance to the KRAs by setting out what needs to be done to realise them. Some activities are routine: to prepare weekly lesson plans and to evaluate the effectiveness of those lessons. Some point to practices that it is hoped or intended will become routine, but clearly are, in a particular school or curriculum area, not yet so: for example, to improve communication with members of staff over content and methodology in a particular curriculum area. Some are specific to a given stage of an innovation and will change in character as

Figure 6.2 Key result areas

TEACHING

CARING

MANAGEMENT

ADMINISTRATION

EXTRACURRICULAR ACTIVITIES

OUTREACH

PERSONAL DEVELOPMENT

For all those KEY RESULT AREAS which are applicable to a teacher at a given stage in his or her career ACTIVITIES can be specified. By selecting certain KEY RESULT AREAS and, within these, certain ACTIVITIES, the appraiser and appraisee will identify the appraisal GOALS.

The APPRAISAL INTERVIEW is a sampling process and the number of goals that can be considered in depth will be limited. The choice of appraisal goals is determined jointly by what will be of value to the appraisee and what will be of value to the institution.

© Routledge 1991

soon as that stage has been attained: for example, to plan and implement for a trial period of two years an equitable system for the allocation under local financial management of resource funding to departments.

There is no upper or lower limit to the number of activities that can or should be devised for any given KRA. The only useful advice is that activities should not be trivialised by multiplicity. It is their quality, not their quantity, which is important. It is, however, essential that they are phrased with absolute clarity and that agreement about their intent exists between appraiser and appraisee. For it is from the key result areas and the related activities that the goals will be educed that will form the main basis of the appraisal process.

AGREEING GOALS

It must be accepted that no appraisal process can possibly be all-embracing. There must be some element of sampling and it is only reasonable that the broad outline of the sample is agreed early on. We have far too often in past examination syllabuses seen attempts to cover so wide a sweep of human knowledge and experience that success is either a lottery or the consequence of some skilled picking of a way through a minefield by a teacher who knows the way the mind of the examiner is likely to work. This is not what appraisal is about. We are seeking through consensus to establish goals which will, on the one hand, improve the quality of performance of the individual teacher and, on the other, raise the standard of what the school has collectively to offer to its clients or stakeholders.

Goalsetting is therefore a matter of establishing priorities with those two aims in mind. Some goals will have higher priority because they will best meet the needs of the individual teacher at this point in time; others because they reflect important stages in the school's development plan. In either case they must be seen, not in isolation, but as part of a continuing developmental process. Furthermore, senior management must identify – and share with staff collectively and individually – the relationship between the two sets of goals.

If in the setting of goals there is an excessive concentration on the task elements of the job specification, then there is a danger of losing out on some of those personal, even idiosyncratic qualities that have made highly memorable a number of teachers with whom many of us will at some time have worked or by whom we have been taught as students. We well remember an art teacher whose weekend party-going invariably left him morose and uncommunicative on a Monday morning. After one more than hectic celebration he arrived for his first class of the week, slumped in his chair and buried his head in his arms. The students knew better than to interrupt; but after twenty minutes one bold spirit ventured to call out 'Sir? Sir? What shall we draw?' 'Draw HELL!' was the reply; and they did.

He was a brilliant and highly successful teacher, whether judged by examination results, displays of work, his cross-curricular influence, his general but unassuming erudition, or his concern for students and the affection in which he was held. It is highly unlikely that he ever presented a set of lesson notes to his head of department, however, or conducted a self-evaluation of any lesson he gave. It would be a pity if the requirements of appraisal led us to diminish such people in favour of wholly task-oriented activities.

Nevertheless, it would be irresponsible to allow the need to recognise and make room for some individuality to blind us to the importance of striking a healthy balance between personal and institutional development. What follows in Figures 6.3 and 6.4 are the first stages of a flowchart which builds up by further stages to the full model which can be seen in Figure 7.2 on page 120.

In goalsetting, then, the individual teacher has identified those areas of the job specification which, for an agreed period, are to be performance priorities. These priorities have been shared with a colleague who has managerial responsibility within the institution at a level which enables her both to be acceptable as a critic of what is being put forward and to be cognisant with the school's development plan and the way in which it is being implemented. The level of seniority required to exercise that

Figure 6.3 Performance appraisal: the process – stage I

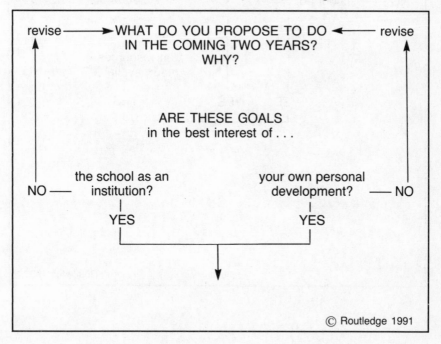

© Routledge 1991

Figure 6.4 Performance appraisal: the process – stage II

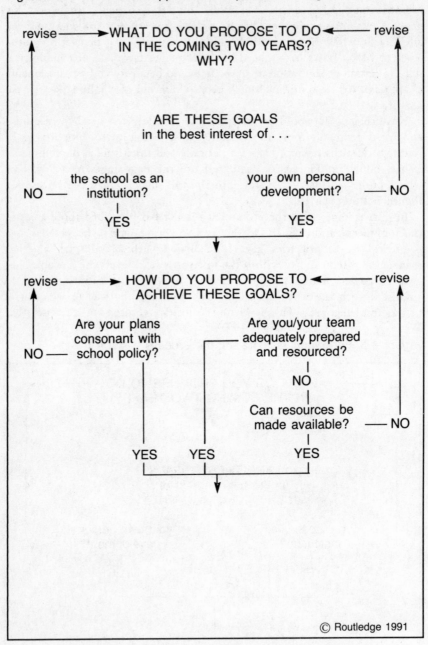

responsibility will vary from school to school and depend on the institution's management style and structure.

Yet goalsetting is incomplete and ineffectual unless the means to the achievement of these goals are also shared. Even though the goals may be mutually acceptable, two serious hindrances to the realisation of these proposals may be revealed as discussion proceeds. The first is that, while the goals themselves may be acceptable, the means of their achievement may not be in accord with school policy. For example, there may be the intention to proceed unilaterally with curriculum developments within a department or a curriculum area which impinge upon possible developments within another department or area. When this comes to light it may have to be pointed out that to act without full discussion with colleagues is contrary to the school's policy of collegiality, however meritorious the goal that has been proposed.

Secondly, discussion may reveal that there are important resource considerations that may affect the realisation of the goals. These may be human resources — an expectation of staffing that cannot at this stage of school planning be guaranteed; or material resources — where a decision to divert funds from what may well be a no less laudable goal proposed by another member of staff might be necessary; or a funding resource from the school's INSET budget, where this claim must be weighed against the as yet unknown totality of potential in-service requirements.

All this may sound very complex but in reality it is no more than sound managerial sense: the parts of the machine must mesh smoothly if the machine as a whole is to function effectively. Accountability demands that senior management takes a holistic or 'helicopter' view of the enterprise; and goals which, viewed in isolation, appear to be sound may not be timely or appropriate for the institution as a whole.

There is a danger in discussing goalsetting, particularly with keen and enterprising members of staff, that their enthusiasm leads senior management to give hostages to fortune: to offer resources or make decisions before the overall pattern of development can be foreseen. This can in part be avoided by having a well established and updated school development plan; but it also requires a certain amount of constraint in planning so that a balanced progression can be maintained. Goalsetting for appraisal is therefore an exercise that must be seen contextually with the audit of the whole school policy; and modifications to that policy, necessary as aspects of the school's development plan are achieved, as new elements are introduced and as priorities change, will have their bearing on individual goals.

ANTICIPATING CONSTRAINTS

If management has to be wary of promising resources at the time of goalsetting before the totality of resources at its disposal is known, then equally it has to recognise that their absence will influence an individual teacher's ability to attain goals. In goalsetting, therefore, there is a need to apply the 'if . . . then' formula now being recognised as crucial to planning by managers who use computer analysis for their budgeting: *if* one set of resource considerations – staffing, time, funding – apply *then* the goals as they stand are achievable; *if* those resources are not available, *then* there will be certain predictable constraints on achievement.

It is possible to make too much of this. Teachers have made bricks without straw for many years now and in any area of human endeavour occasional and unpredicted – often unpredictable – obstacles are just another challenge to professionals well used to challenges. Nevertheless, it is only fair to appraiser and appraisee that those potential constraints which can be anticipated are noted at the time of goalsetting. It is clearly good management to be able to anticipate problems and to include in goalsetting some contingency planning, rather than to learn that what might have been a minor and removable obstacle has become an unclimbable wall.

Figure 6.5 Contingency planning

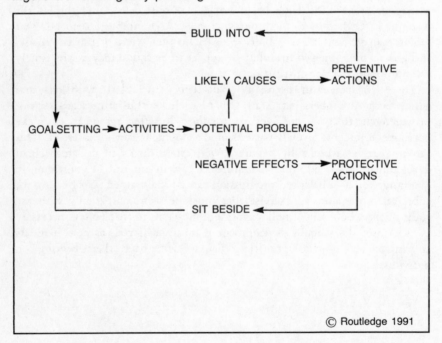

CONTINGENCY PLANNING

This strategy, widely used in management planning, has a key part to play in goalsetting. As Figure 6.5 suggests, it is not enough to identify the key activities which will give substance to the goals. It is also wise to attempt some identification of the problems that are likely to arise in the process of realising these goals. There are two kinds of problem. There are those which can be anticipated and prevented; and there are those which would lead to a need to modify the plan.

The first kind of problem can be illustrated as follows. If the goal of a curriculum postholder was a major curriculum review in the light of the developments required by the National Curriculum and that teacher was not taking advantage of the reviews taking place concurrently in other curriculum areas, might not some excellent opportunities for cross-curricular planning be missed? Raising this potential problem may suggest to a curriculum postholder the advisability of sharing with other curriculum postholders the review stage by stage and not, as might have been originally decided, when the task had been completed. A better, more collaborative way of working is therefore built back into the plan.

The second kind of problem can be illustrated thus. Meeting this same goal by an agreed time may well be dependent on the availability of certain resources: of materials, of information, of time, of training. Without this availability, there would clearly be a negative effect on the achievement of the task, and it would have to be recognised that the goal was incapable of being realised unless those who controlled these resources recognised their responsibility for the success of the enterprise.

Not all potential problems can be readily identified in advance and their harmful consequences negated by improvements to the original plan. Some potential problems may be no more than hypotheses: if the school were unable to fill the staffing vacancy which has just arisen with someone with certain skills, then it might be necessary to consider the release of a member of staff from one of the goals recently agreed since he is the only remaining member of staff with these skills. This protective action will then sit alongside the plan, ready for implementation should the contingency arise. Examples like these emphasise the close relationship between individual goalsetting decisions and school management considerations.

CONTRACTING

Goalsetting should always end with a written contract. Whether the compilation of the contract is the task of the appraiser or the appraisee is immaterial. What is important is that it represents a consensus view on what has been decided and that it includes all constraints that have been identified and any contingency actions that have been foreshadowed. If there is no contract, then there is no point of reference about what goals have been agreed. Memory alone is not a good management tool.

MONITORING

It would be absurd to go from goalsetting at the beginning of the process to appraisal at the end without any intermediate checkpoints. This is not because people will not work without being 'coerced, controlled and directed' – the Theory X view of motivation posited by McGregor (1960); rather it is because probably the highest of all motivational factors is the recognition by superiors and colleagues of achievement together with the preparedness to help with the removal of obstacles to that achievement.

Schools are institutions in which there ought to be every opportunity for regular and sustained human contact, yet the cellular nature of the classrooms in many of our primary and secondary schools has reinforced the traditional autonomy of the profession. Monitoring, however 'light touch', may be thought of as an intrusion on a private domain and to be avoided. Consequently, even though schools have become far more corporate institutions in recent years, many managers in education are still slow to commend their teachers, though they may go to great lengths to devise forms of recognition for student achievement. 'He was an excellent head to work for', reflected a teacher we knew well, 'and his staff knew that he valued them highly. Yet he rarely, if ever, was heard to say so. We were not looking for praise, but an occasional indication of his appreciation of our worth would have done much for our morale when for any reason we were in the doldrums.' Whether or not this teacher was aware of it, he was talking about the fourth of the five levels of needs in Maslow's theory of human motivation (1959): 'ego' or esteem needs.

In the appraisal process, monitoring should never be left to chance. It needs to be built into the agreed procedures. No one would wish to be so pedantic as to specify that a senior or middle manager is required to monitor once every ten days those for whom he is managerially responsible; yet it is important that a review of progress takes place at agreed intervals and is not left to the chance meeting. It is plainly not enough to pass someone in the corridor with a breezy 'Everything going all right then?' This approach hardly gives the other much opportunity to say 'No, I need to discuss what is now going wrong with those goals we set so thoroughly at our last meeting'.

In some situations shared concerns can be voiced in departmental and other relatively small meetings, provided time is made available on the agenda; but the provision of opportunities of this kind does not obviate the need for regular one-to-one discussions where the manager can act as facilitator for her colleague so that his appraisal goals can the better be attained. The further we get into the role of the appraiser, the more it becomes clear that, among the interpersonal skills that are required, counselling occupies a prime place.

TRAINING FOR GOALSETTING

The job specifications on the following pages come from two schools, one secondary, the other primary. Each job specification is offered not primarily as a model, but rather as a training opportunity for work in groups in order to translate the responsibilities into key result areas and activities, and then to identify goals. In both cases the job specification is, as it stands, generic. In the secondary school there are two similar posts, one with responsibility for pupils of years 7–9, the other for years 10–11. In the primary school job specification, the headteacher has chosen a common form of words which will identify the curriculum area of the postholder only when the line 'curriculum coordinator for . . .' is completed. The training tasks are, it will be observed, almost identical for both phases.

If this training exercise is taking place within a school, then the actual job specification of a comparable postholder can be used and the activities, both routine and innovatory, will be those genuinely identified as appropriate to the needs of the school and the status of the post. If the training exercise takes place within an LEA, then a job specification and school situation derived from one of the schools in the workshop can be used. In both cases some pre-planning is necessary.

However these case studies are used, it is valuable to have an independent observer to comment on both the conduct and the outcomes of the negotiation that takes place. One potential danger is that of over-commitment in goalsetting. If goals are to be realised, then they must be realisable. This implies that time management must be a consideration in the negotiation. Surprisingly, perhaps, it is often necessary for the appraiser to remind the appraisee of this constraint, both in role-play and in real life!

CONCLUSION

Probably the most regrettable consequence of the recommendation that appraisal be biennial is that the normal cycle of the class teacher's goalsetting always has been and always will be annual. Most primary teachers and all secondary teachers will have new classes and therefore new challenges which may well lead to the need to conclude one set of goals and establish another. Thus, even though appraisal may be biennial, goalsetting may not. It would seem to us likely that the formal follow-up session recommended by the NSG will in practice, for goals related to teaching key result areas, become more like a halfway stage mini-appraisal. For some goals, needless to say, in particular those related to administrative and managerial activities, the two-year span is reasonable; but it would be a sad day for the profession if appraisal of the central activity of the school, the promotion of the learning process, were in any way debased or marginalised.

Job specification: secondary

HEADS OF SCHOOL

Job purpose: to create and maintain the highest possible standard of academic achievement and pastoral welfare for the year groups designated.

Responsibilities

Pupil progress:
- Liaison with academic heads on progress.
- Monitoring pupil progress and taking appropriate action: input into the RoA and pupil review/report documents; general over-sight of the maintenance of these documents.
- Overall responsibility for the conduct of examinations within their section of the school.

Pupil welfare:
The principal aim must be to create an atmosphere of hard work and positive care and consideration by and for pupils within the designated years by:
- Ensuring that pupil behaviour is in accordance with the aims and code of behaviour of the school;
- Ensuring that pupils' appearance is within the standard set by the school's uniform regulations;
- Coordinating and leading the work of form tutors and supporting them in all aspects of their work; holding regular meetings of tutors and making copies of minutes available to the senior staff;
- Undertaking overall responsibility for liaison with parents and external social and welfare agencies;
- Organising parental consultation evenings/sessions;
- Holding pupil records and ensuring transfer of information to other schools/courts/employers etc as appropriate;
- Making arrangements for assemblies;
- Overseeing arrangements and activities for non-assembly time: social and study skills, tutor programmes and collective worship; and for social and charitable events.

General:
Heads of School are members of the senior management team and of the academic board. In addition, regular liaison and consultation with the headteacher and the deputies concerning all aspects of their work are essential.

© Routledge 1991

Instructions

TASK 1

Decide as a group whether you wish to work on the job specification of the Head of Lower School (years 7–9) or Head of Middle School (years 10–11). This done, identify from three to five additional **specific** responsibilities which the groups wishes to be added to the job description. Now translate these responsibilities, both generic and specific, into KRAs.

TASK 2

Divide into two subgroups, one representing the headteacher, the other the Head of School. In each subgroup identify a number of **activities** relating to each KRA. Some will be maintenance activities; some will be developmental or innovatory activities. Since the actual stage of development of the school is unknown, each subgroup will have to hypothesise the latter activities.

TASK 3

The two subgroups now meet to compare and agree the activities in each KRA and to identify those goals on which the Head of School will be appraised at the end of the period under review. This is best done in role-play, with one person from each subgroup now representing the headteacher and the Head of School.

Job specification: primary

CURRICULUM COORDINATOR FOR _____

In addition to teaching his/her own class in accordance with the approaches to discovery-based learning laid down in the school curriculum policy:

- to be responsible for updating all class teachers in the curriculum area for which he/she is designated as coordinator;
- to develop and maintain suitable curriculum materials in that area;
- to promote the sharing by class teachers of knowledge and experience of curriculum content and methodology in that area;
- to explore ways of involving parents and members of the community in contributing to the curriculum in that area;
- to communicate information about the development of the curriculum to the headteacher;

and further:

- to contribute to the development of a caring school community in which there is equality of opportunity regardless of sex or ethnic origin;
- to promote a moral climate in which there is respect for property and the views of others.

Instructions

TASK 1

Decide as a group which curriculum area you will allocate to the curriculum coordinator whose job specification you have before you. This done, identify from two to four additional **specific** reponsibilities which the group wishes to be added to the job description. Now translate these responsibilities, both generic and specific, into KRAs.

TASK 2

Divide into two subgroups, one representing the headteacher, the other the curriculum coordinator. In each subgroup identify a number of **activities** relating to each KRA. Some will be maintenance activities; some will be development or innovatory activities. Since the actual stage of development of the school is unknown, each subgroup will have to hypothesise the latter activities.

TASK 3

The two subgroups now meet to compare and agree the activities in each KRA and to identify those goals on which the curriculum coordinator will be appraised at the end of the period under review. This is best done in role-play, with one person from each subgroup now representing the headteacher and the curriculum coordinator.

Chapter 7

The appraisal interview

If the appraisal interview is seen as no more than a stage in the process that began with goalsetting and has continued through monitoring and counselling, then it should contain no surprises. Nevertheless, it may seem to the appraisee to be a more threatening activity than any that has preceded it. However much it has been emphasised that the whole appraisal process is about individual and institutional improvement and not about assessment, there will always be some who perceive it as judgmental; and this stage, coming as it does as the conclusion of the cycle, will lend credence to any misgivings that the purpose of appraisal might, after all, be summative. It follows, therefore, that preparation for the appraisal interview must be thorough, and must emphasise that appraiser and appraisee are engaging in a joint activity, each with a responsibility for preparing in order to ensure that the outcomes are as valuable as possible.

PREPARATION BY APPRAISER

The appraiser needs to prepare herself in a number of ways. First, she must go back to the record of the goalsetting discussion which began the process, both to remind herself of what was agreed and to see the goals afresh in the light of what has transpired in the intervening months. Constraints, the strength of which may have become more obvious during periodic discussions, have to be reviewed for the effect they may have had on original goals; or, if they have been overcome, for the time and energy costs on the individual teacher.

The general period of appraisal interviews, in most schools likely to be concentrated into a two-month time span, has a way of highlighting interconnections that might otherwise have gone unnoticed: the degree of success in meeting a particular goal in one area of the institution has often a knock-on effect, for good or ill, on another area. Thus a highly successful development of social activities for parents undertaken as a goal by one teacher may have led to an improvement in relationships between parents and staff in general and contributed greatly to more effective communication over curriculum content and methodology. Alternatively, an in-service day ill-conceived and inadequately prepared by one member of staff may have undermined the ability of curriculum leaders in general to generate enthusiasm among staff for their concerns over the implementation of the National Curriculum.

Next, and particularly in the large school, the appraiser needs to assemble information about the appraisee's performance. It is crucial that this is indeed fact and not opinion, however difficult it may be in practice to distinguish between them. 'Your Year Head thinks that you have not been pulling your weight recently' is the kind of remark that might easily come out in the appraisal interview; but phrased thus it will almost certainly lead a teacher to whom it is made to conclude that he is indeed being judged, and on hearsay evidence at that. However, the same preparation could well have resulted in the statement 'I understand you have recently had some discussion with your Year Head about your strengths and weaknesses as a tutor. Since improvement in this area was, I recall, one of your goals, should we not discuss this further?' This would be an unexceptionable and far more effective use of information received by the appraiser. It would also emphasise the appraisee's responsibility to the Year Head for meeting the goal.

It is vital that preparing for the appraisal interview in this way, however large the school or complex its organisation, is not left until the last minute, but is part of the continuous monitoring process that every school manager should engage in. The dictum 'There should be no surprises' applies to the whole range of the appraisal process; and the communication flow within the school should alert any member of staff with managerial responsibility to strengths and weaknesses as they arise. If the appraiser is hearing of these only at the time of the appraisal interview, then there is decidedly something wrong with the system. Nevertheless, there is clearly a need for the appraiser at this time to review her perceptions of those aspects of performance for which she is not directly responsible by talking to those members of staff who are, both to ensure that she is fully updated and to alert them to their vicarious involvement in the interview.

THE AGENDA

Preparation leads naturally into building the agenda for the interview. We feel strongly that anything much beyond an hour for the interview is likely to be counterproductive. This is not an *ex cathedra* opinion, but one borne out in many review day discussions with teachers at our workshops after they have engaged in appraisal trialling in their schools. Some have acknowledged that preparation which they thought was adequate but which has proved not to be has been the main reason why they exceeded the time limit they set themselves: they have been too easily side-tracked; taken by surprise by information that has been disclosed by the appraisee of which they were not aware; been oblivious to the intensity of feeling that has been generated by some incident. Yet by far the commonest cause of the overlong interview is the simplest: the desire to leave no stone unturned, no avenue unexplored.

Planning the content

The agenda for the appraisal interview must be selective. The goals which have been set at the beginning of the appraisal process provide the broad ground from which that selection may be made; they are not of themselves the agenda. In a general introductory item of the agenda, confined by agreement to no more than 5 minutes, certain activities identified in the goalsetting session may easily be cleared out of the way.

Establishing rapport

Dealing with reassuring, non-controversial matters helps considerably to establish rapport:

> It seems to me that staff are well satisfied with the new arrangements for access to resource materials that you have instituted. Have you also had favourable feedback?

> Parents have commented favourably on the new appointments system you introduced this year for report discussions. What is your impression?

These are not bromides. Rapport is *not* established by asking questions or making statements easily recognised by the appraisee as meaningless or insignificant. The questions asked at this stage are, however, those that you do not expect to give rise to discussion in depth. Yet, despite full preparation, it can happen that a matter that the appraiser expects to deal with cursorily in the interview suddenly becomes a matter of greater moment. In such a situation the appraiser will have to decide what action to take: to propose that this item be added to the agenda proper, recognising that it may then disconcert the appraisee by replacing another for which the appraisee had prepared; or to suggest that it be discussed further outside the appraisal interview itself. It is important that the appraisal interview itself deals with matters relevant to appraisal. There is a danger that it becomes another discussion on management issues for which there are other occasions and quite possibly more appropriate forums.

Planning the agenda

In planning the agenda it is as well to estimate that no main item is likely to take less than 10 minutes and may well take 15 minutes. Bearing in mind that time will also need to be allocated for other key elements of the appraisal interview, three – at most four – goals will be as many as can comfortably be reviewed. How and by whom should they be selected?

If appraisal is to be a process of negotiation and sharing, then part of that choice should lie with the appraisee. Not only does this signal that his own perceptions of the appraisal process are important to the appraiser, it also introduces a concept of interdependence and mutuality upon which long-term confidence is built. It is possible for the appraisee to include an item in which he feels that he has been less successful than he would have wished or expected, in order to indicate that, given more support or resources, he would have achieved more. Of course there will be some who may appear to have chosen items for the agenda in order to engage in buck-passing or trumpet-blowing. Far from considering this a disadvantage or an abuse of the 'privilege' of contributing to the agenda, we believe that it is healthy that the appraiser be non-judgmental in such a situation. What may appear to be buck-passing can sometimes be a genuine confusion over accountability roles. Trumpet-blowing may indicate that there has been a failure somewhere to recognise and praise achievement. What often happens in practice, though, is that an item the appraiser is herself desirous of seeing on the agenda is proposed by the appraisee, reinforcing her view that this is an item of mutual concern.

The concept of mutuality referred to above is of vital importance in appraisal. If appraisal is to contribute to school improvement then it must strive to avoid win–lose situations; and there is no better way of doing this than to accept and demonstrate from the outset that the appraisee/appraiser relationship is not one of subordinate/superordinate but rather of two colleagues seeking mutually acceptable outcomes. In one sense, therefore, in the interview each party may at any given moment be in either role. 'Had you supported me in such a way, I might well have achieved greater success in meeting this goal' is, if accepted as a valid criticism by the appraiser, just such a role reversal.

The agreed agenda

This should be in the hands of the appraisee in good time before the interview: at least 48 hours in normal circumstances. There is no need, in a negotiated agenda, for a catchall item of Any Other Business. This is not the kind of occasion on which any last-minute item is likely to need to be included. Indeed, introduced by either appraiser or appraisee, it would seem to be more of a device to engender suspicion or promote discord and therefore quite alien to the atmosphere in which an appraisal interview is best conducted.

Figure 7.1 Preparation for appraisal

BEFORE THE APPRAISAL INTERVIEW ...

THE APPRAISER NEEDS TO:

       REVIEW
       agreed goals

       IDENTIFY
       potential constraints
       related school developments

       ASSEMBLE
       information

       SHARE AND PREPARE
       agenda items

THE APPRAISEE NEEDS TO:

       REVIEW
       personal progress (self-appraisal)

       SHARE AND PREPARE
       agenda items

APPRAISER AND APPRAISEE NEED TO:

       AGREE
       location of interview
       time allocation
       recording

Controlling the agenda

To do this without stifling discussion or riding roughshod over a colleague's opinions is not easy; and there will for some years to come be many teachers newly assigned the role of appraiser who will have had little experience of this skill, certainly in a one-to-one situation. It is better, if it appears that the planned time is likely to be overrun, to pause and agree which item on the agenda cannot be satisfactorily explored in the remaining time and should be left for an occasion outside the appraisal interview itself; alternatively, if there is any feeling that this is an item that must be discussed within the appraisal interview, to agree to meet again to conclude the agenda.

PREPARATION BY APPRAISEE

In his teaching the good teacher is constantly going through a process of self-evaluation. Did I achieve my lesson objectives? Did I communicate successfully? Did I pay sufficient attention to the full range of ability within the class? Did I avoid sex stereotyping in my examples? Did I give enough time and the right sort of help to pupils with special needs? Did I get feedback from the class on the outcomes of the lesson? This is not to suggest that he routinely catechises himself with these and other questions. The beginner teacher may and should from time to time; but the experienced teacher has an intuitive feel for the consequences of his teaching and knows where there have been strengths and weaknesses.

Classroom observation, it is widely recognised, is effective not so much for the contribution of the observer as for the heightened self-perceptions of the teacher. This is no less true of the appraisal interview itself. Here, however, we are dealing with a complexity of goals and not simply the aims and objectives of a single lesson; and, because the time span is greater, there is the need for a more formal framework for self-appraisal. The proforma on pages 112–13 derives, with only minor modifications, from Annex B of the ACAS agreement (1986). That agreement underpinned much of the thinking and work of the pilot appraisal projects.

The questions that appear on the proforma are both retrospective, in that they look back to the previous goalsetting activity, and prospective, in that they begin to identify ways in which goals will be carried forward, revised and renewed in the next review period and, to some extent, the means by which they will be achieved. Important though it is to both appraiser and appraisee that there is a recognisable relationship between the present appraisal interview and future goals, it is essential that the next phase of goalsetting does not dominate the discussion. Goalsetting is a discrete activity and should not intrude unduly on the appraisal of past performance.

Self-appraisal: interview preparation proforma

What do you consider to be the main tasks and responsibilities of your current post?

In the period under review, what aspects of your work have given you the greatest satisfaction?

And the least satisfaction?

Did anything prevent you from achieving what you had intended to do?

Have these obstacles been removed? If not, how might they be removed?

© Routledge 1991

Are there any changes in the school organisation which might help you to improve your performance?

What in your view should be your main goals for the next review period?

What help do you need to this end? From whom?

How do you envisage your career developing?

Any other comments?

The questions merit some detailed comment:

What do you consider to be the main tasks and responsibilities of your current post?

The ways in which appraisees approach this question are, in our experience, many and varied. This does not vitiate the question, for, fortunately, nobody is concerned about comparing or evaluating responses. The main purpose of the question is to enable the appraisee rapidly to identify the areas which will be under review in the appraisal process. In schools where the phrase 'key result areas' has already been absorbed into the accepted language of appraisal, it can be either substituted for or understood by 'main tasks and responsibilities'.

In the period under review, what aspects of your work have given you the greatest satisfaction? And the least satisfaction?

It is important to observe that this question asks about *satisfaction* rather than *success*. This approach emphasises that the central purpose of appraisal is not assessment but personal development. Self-actualisation, as Maslow (1959) terms it, is the highest level motivator in his needs hierarchy.

Did anything prevent you from achieving what you had intended to do? Have these obstacles been removed? If not, how might they be removed?

Here the appraisee has the opportunity to reflect on constraints on his performance. Some of these will undoubtedly have been identified as potential constraints at the goalsetting stage; but others will have surfaced in the period under review. The second question reaffirms the mutuality of the appraisal process by inviting the appraisee to consider the causes of the constraints. There is no attempt in this section to identify whether or not it has lain within the power of the appraisee himself to deal with the obstacles. This can best be considered during the appraisal interview itself. What the questions are likely to do, however, is to stimulate some self-perceptions which will prepare the ground for a profitable appraisal interview.

Are there any changes in the school organisation which might help you to improve your performance?

The relationship between personal performance and school organisation is crucial, but often underestimated by those in managerial roles. While the annual review process or audit increasingly being used in schools gives staff the opportunity to reflect on the nexus between school organisation and staff performance in general, the appraisal process offers a rare opportunity for considering how personal performance is enhanced or inhibited by school organisation.

What in your view should be your main goals for the next review period? What help do you need to this end? From whom?

The appraisal interview is not the goalsetting interview. Nevertheless, since the appraisal process is cyclical it is inevitable that goals will begin to emerge. In some cases it will be immediately apparent that a goal remains constant from one year to the next though the emphasis – and consequently the activity – may change, perhaps from innovation to consolidation. In other cases it may be judged at the appraisal interview that the goal has been achieved, at least to the extent that it has now become a routine activity. New goals and major developments from existing KRAs are likely to feature in the appraisee's thinking in response to the first question in this section; the importance of support mechanisms is highlighted by the second and third.

How do you envisage your career developing?

There are those who argue that career development reviews should be kept quite distinct from the appraisal process. One secondary headteacher with whom we have worked, who had before engaging in appraisal training built up an extensive and well structured programme of staff development interviews, took the view that it would be both impractical and time-consuming to maintain two distinct processes and holds that this question is crucial to the appraisal process. In his earlier work on staff appraisal in Nottinghamshire, Chris Saville, now Chief Education Officer for Avon, created what he called a 'professional development model', an appraisal flowchart within which there lay a 'nodal point'. That nodal point offers the consideration of six broad possibilities for career development: secondment; task specific secondment; retraining; retirement; other [i.e. non-teaching] activity or work; and job change. Within that last category there lies a host of alternatives: for example, lateral transfer, teacher exchange, a change of post within the same institution, additional responsibilities, movement to a different institution (Nottinghamshire LEA, 1985). With promotion prospects blocked for many secondary teachers in their mid-career years, it is an important part of appraisal that other possibilities are opened up. For some members of staff this question in the self-appraisal proforma will be only of passing interest. For others, however, it will act as a powerful trigger to the appraisal of future professional status or even reveal hidden disquiet about present role or status. That the question itself is a valid part of the appraisal process we have no doubt. It is, however, up to the appraiser to decide whether or not the time available in the interview permits the matter to be discussed in the detail it warrants or whether, after an initial airing of it, it might not better be discussed on another occasion. Furthermore, particularly in a secondary school of any size, the question may well arise as to whether the appraiser is the right person with whom this matter can usefully be discussed. Much depends on how, in such schools, decisions are made on who will appraise whom. This is a point which will be taken up later in the chapter.

Sharing the self-appraisal

Finally, there is the question of whether or not a copy of the self-appraisal proforma should be made available to the appraiser before the interview. The ACAS document recommends that the decision be left to the appraisee. We can see no circumstance in which it would not be helpful for the document to be made available, provided appraisal is viewed by both parties as a collaborative and not a confrontational activity. There is likely to be much in the document that will contribute to the building up of a mutually acceptable agenda; and there will also be indicators as to which items on the agenda deserve the fullest treatment and the greatest alloca- tion of time. There may also be signals to the appraiser of facts that she should ascertain or areas that she should investigate before the meeting.

PREPARING THE INTERVIEW

As with the goalsetting interview, the location depends on both the availability of suitable venues and the wishes of appraiser and appraisee. However, in this case it is more important that the venue is one that can be safeguarded from interruption, by telephone, by visitors, by accidental intrusion, by crises. There will be schools, particularly primary schools, where the appropriate privacy is hard to find. Even in large secondary schools, where offices and similar rooms are more commonly available, there may well be a reluctance on the part of some members of staff to surrender their room, such are the proprietorial attitudes to space in some institutions. Venues for appraisal should therefore not be dealt with on a casual basis, but be planned with the same precision and attention to detail that schools apply to the allocation of rooms for governors' meetings, staff appointment interviews and school examinations. In addition, it would be sensible for this issue to be included on the agenda of a general staff meeting at a time when other appraisal issues were being discussed.

We have already indicated that an hour is the optimum time for an appraisal interview. This said, however, it is wise to allocate the room for a longer period: a further ten minutes before and again after the intended hour. This allows for the seating to be arranged in a way that suits the occasion: informally, with eye contact but not eyeball to eyeball, and at the same level so that no hidden messages about status are conveyed. A small table is useful, since both appraiser and appraisee almost certainly have papers which they will not want to clutch throughout the meeting.

Time after the allocated hour is also important. Sometimes, even in training situations, there is a good deal of tension in the air, however well the appraisal interview has gone, and the appraiser will be wise to dissipate this with some general conversation. To expect the appraisee, mind buzzing with all that has been discussed, to go straight from the interview to teach is not advisable, though sometimes it will be inevitable.

Nor is it only in the appraisee's interest that some time is available for unwinding. Particularly while the appraiser is relatively inexperienced in appraisal interviewing, there will be occasions when she will find merit in seeking the appraisee's perceptions, while the details are fresh in the minds of both, of the way the interview was conducted. Even with experienced interviewers this strategy may be psychologically sound in that it switches the focus of attention from appraisee to appraiser, a move which in itself lessens tension for both of them.

In training workshops during a final 'Any Questions?' plenary the question has often been raised about the merits or demerits of the presence at the interview of a third party, as non-participatory observer. It can be argued that the presence of this third party radically alters the relationship between appraiser and appraisee. However self-effacing that observer tries to be, however well the role has been clarified, it is still possible that, by the nature of his standing in the school, he will appear to relate more closely to one party than the other: as appraisee's 'friend' perhaps, with undertones of the practices of disciplinary hearings; or as second appraiser. The stance that we have taken in our workshops is, in general, to advise against it. Yet it is only right that we should record differences of opinion among experienced colleagues. One primary headteacher who had introduced routine appraisal into his school some time before it became a major national innovation included an observer in the interviewing process and maintains that this proved to be a means of reducing, not heightening tension: the observer was seen by both parties as a moderating influence on the process. Another headteacher, more recently trialling for the first time appraisal interviews in his secondary school where there was already a well-established practice of staff development reviews, introduced the observer with staff agreement in order that his appraisal team might be able to learn from an objective monitoring of the process. At the end of this trialling phase, somewhat to his surprise, there was staff unanimity that there was so much merit in the presence of the observer that the practice should be continued beyond the trialling stage. There is, as both headteachers have readily recognised, a considerable time-cost in this practice which they might not be able to meet without a deleterious effect on other demands on that most valuable of resources. Nobody, it is agreed, should introduce this procedure without full consideration of its immediate and long-term implications.

RECORDING

A report on the appraisal interview is obligatory. For any report to be compiled there must be some kind of record made of the interview. It should be factual, objective, non-judgmental and open: vital if teachers are not to suspect that the appraisal process has hidden motives or purposes.

It is highly unlikely that tape-recording the appraisal interview would be acceptable to the teaching profession even though it would provide a verbatim record of the discussion. In training, most teachers do not find the presence of a tape recorder inhibiting, somewhat contrary to their expectation. However, with appraisal beyond the voluntary and exploratory stage, a tape-recording may pose a very real threat, to the appraiser no less than the appraisee, since its existence gives rise to a host of delicate questions. Who has the right of access to it? For how long will it be kept? How will it be safeguarded? Perhaps the most relevant question is the rather cynical one: what is the point since who will have the time to listen to it?

Notetaking

The taking of notes, on the other hand, is to be expected, since few appraisers will have the confidence to rely on memory alone. It will happen that, while the appraisee is talking, a question comes into the appraiser's mind that she would like to raise next and which she wishes to note before it is forgotten. Or it may be that a matter is raised that needs further exploration outside the interview. For such matters a word or phrase jotted down will suffice, though it is as well to accompany the action with a comment, such as 'I am just making a note of that'.

There is also a need to note those rather more substantive matters which are to be included in the contract, to which we refer in the next section. Some appraisers will be skilled enough to do this also 'on the hoof', by means of brief reminders. Others will prefer to make a definite break, for example, at the end of an agenda item, saying: 'Just give me a moment to write a comment on what we have been talking about.' Some will even like to share this note there and then with the appraisee. Quakers conduct their business meetings in this way, the clerk writing up each minute and seeking the meeting's agreement to the wording as each agenda item is concluded. There can then be no doubt about consensus.

There is, we have found, even in school trialling of appraisal, a good deal of suspicion over the purpose of notetaking and many headteachers have told us that the only satisfactory way of defusing potential hostility is to clarify the purpose of notetaking with the staff as a whole at the earliest possible stage in the introduction of appraisal. It is important that it be emphasised that these notes do not form part of any dossier but have one function only, to prompt the appraiser's memory. Some headteachers have gone so far as to undertake that appraisers will destroy all notes once their immediate purpose has been fulfilled.

It might well be thought that to go further than this in assurance is unnecessary. Nevertheless, many workshop members have had the experience that, even after these undertakings, there is still merit in reiterating the agreement at the beginning of each appraisal interview, when the tension of the situation may be at its peak. A demonstration of open behaviour costs nothing and is a good contribution to the building of rapport, particularly until such time as appraisal procedures have become well established and have ceased to ring alarm bells.

CONTRACTING

Every appraisal interview will give rise to some issues for future action on the part of appraiser or appraisee that need to be recorded in the form of an agreement or contract. There is a need to indicate: those areas for a future goalsetting discussion that have been identified in the interview; issues which involve third parties; undertakings to look at possibilities for in-service training or to examine the resource implications of suggestions that have been made. Appraisers, even if they are headteachers, should always beware of agreeing in the interview to the provision of resources, whether of time or money, until it is possible to collate the needs of all staff and make considered judgments of relative needs. If they do not, then they are offering hostages to fortune, satisfying some at the risk of alienating others.

Even if agreement were reached at the end of each agenda item, the complete contract will not have been written up and agreed during the interview itself. It is advisable, therefore, for the appraiser at the end of the interview to review rapidly from her notes the items which she proposes to include in the document, make sure that there are no omissions and reassure the appraisee that the draft will be cleared with him and a copy provided when it has been typed up.

The document is intended both to be factual and to deal with proposed future actions: to be in effect a checklist whereby both parties can ascertain that what has been promised has in fact been done or, if not, the reasons for inaction investigated. Yet inevitably there will arise situations in which what the contract contains reflects back to omissions or shortcomings which must not be glossed over. It is to be hoped that the atmosphere in the school is that of mutual trust so that it is accepted that what appears is for

Figure 7.2 Performance appraisal: the process – final stage

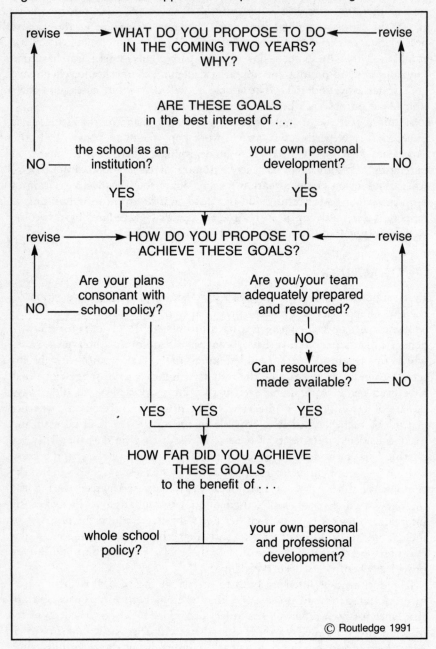

the benefit of both the school and the individual. The now completed performance flow chart in Figure 7.2 emphasises once more the importance of the balance between the individual appraisals and the school development plan.

TRAINING FOR INTERVIEWING

We have used simulation extensively in our appraisal training workshops. All the case studies that appear in this chapter have been trialled frequently in workshops with clientele varying from LEA appraisal training coordinators, officers and advisers to headteachers, staff teams, school staff development coordinators and interested individuals. The case studies are factually based, though the circumstances have always been modified sufficiently to ensure that there can be no identification of their origins. Each newly devised case study has been assessed by us and teams of LEA tutors with whom we have worked in order to identify and amend any area where the text might be misunderstood or misinterpreted. All have been updated from time to time to maintain their contemporaneity. Trainers are at liberty to use these case studies as they stand, to adapt them to suit the circumstances of their LEA or school or to model their own simulations on them.

The case studies are used as follows:

- Groups of four to six participants produce the best results. However, the total number of workshop members or the availability of sufficient tutors may necessitate larger groups.
- Although primary and secondary teachers may with advantage attend the same workshop, for this training activity it is better if the groups are homogeneous.
- To each pair of such groups an appropriate case study is distributed. To one group of the pair is allocated the collective role of appraiser, to the other that of appraisee. It is important that no early decision is made within either group over who will eventually role-play the appraisal interview.
- For each pair of groups there is a tutor to act as facilitator. In order to set up a scenario that is open to a wide range of interpretations the information in the hand-out is deliberately kept to a minimum. The function of the tutor is therefore to negotiate any desired information from one group to the other. The first case study at the end of this chapter will serve as an example. No attempt has been made in it to describe the domestic situation of Gerry Manners. It is therefore open to the appraisee group to devise some personal details that suit the character that is evolving and to use the tutor to convey this information to the appraiser group. It will sometimes happen that the tutor is

charged with conveying information which proves to be unacceptable to the other group: for example, that certain promises to provide resources were made by the headteacher but not adhered to. The appraiser group has the right in this circumstance to refuse to accept the information as it stands and it is the task of the tutor to mediate until there is agreement. Occasionally mediation gives way to arbitration in the interests of the training exercise. One of the key roles of the tutor is to ensure that the preparation for the appraisal interview does not become competitive.

- It will soon become apparent that both groups will have need of the goals that were set earlier in the academic year. There are three possible strategies:

  - They can be provided by the tutor.
  - The appraiser group undertakes to draft them and obtain the appraisee group's agreement that they fairly represent the goals implicit in the text of the case study.
  - One representative of each group is delegated to undertake this as a collaborative task while their colleagues continue with other planning.

The first strategy may be necessary if training time is at a premium. The second and third strategies make for better training. The third will save time but depends on the degree of trust that exists between the groups.

- The appraisee group will now become anxious to see the agenda for the interview and the production of this then becomes a priority for the appraiser group. At the same time the appraiser group will be expecting to see the completed self-appraisal proforma. The discussion within each group as these documents are drafted by the one party and considered by the other will do much to identify and clarify for the workshop members the skills needed to achieve effective outcomes from the interview.

- Each case study will be seen to contain weaknesses as well as strengths, on the part of both the appraisee and other members of staff, including even the appraiser. This underlines the point made earlier that in the appraisal interview the appraiser/appraisee roles may at any given moment be reversed, as failures of management, for example, are revealed.

- A minimum of 90 minutes is required for preparation of the appraisal interview. In two-day workshops it is helpful if the programme can be so arranged that the case study preparation is the concluding session of the first day. This practice has two advantages: the first that the time allocation can sometimes be exceeded by general agreement; the second that rough drafts of the agenda or the self-appraisal proforma can be tidied up overnight by a public-spirited group member and photocopied for distribution to the members of the two groups. A further 15 minutes on the second day can be allocated for last minute thoughts and particularly, if the decision can be held off until this stage, for the choice of role-player from each group.

The role-play

- Those who have elected – or been selected – to play the roles of appraiser and appraisee need a short time to talk to each other in private. This will serve in part to clear up any minor details, for example to agree the names of members of staff who are likely to be referred to in the interview, and in part to allow them to wind down some of the tension that will inevitably have built up. During this time the tutor will ensure that the scene is set for the interview as planned by the appraiser group, with such furniture as is available. Appraiser and appraisee need to be reminded that, although they will be talking to each other, they need to project their voices sufficiently to enable the observers of the role-play to hear them clearly.
- It is advisable to allow 90 minutes for the session. Half of this is for the role-play, half for the discussion which follows. Role-players are often initially aghast that they are expected to keep going for up to 45 minutes, often claiming that in reality there would be much more factual and firsthand evidence on which to call. Our experience is that very rarely does a role-play not fill up this time allocation and often it goes beyond. It is good practice, therefore, for the tutor to have arranged beforehand a 'two minute warning' signal to the appraiser that will enable her to draw the interview to a conclusion. Some tutor control is needed because there are always judgments to be made about the value of the experience that is being observed against the needs of observers to discuss what they have been observing.
- During the role-play those who have been members of the groups take on observational roles. On pages 126–7 will be found an observation schedule. Although practised observers may well be able to cover the whole schedule, most workshop members will not have this degree of expertise. While the appraiser and appraisee are making their final preparations, therefore, the observers decide on which sections of the schedule each will concentrate.
- The tutor will also be observing, mainly in order to be able to guide and prompt, if necessary, the discussion session which follows. Some skilled tutors have the capacity to make rapid notes of the general tenor of each contribution set against a rough time log to be able to show what proportion of the total time was spent on each agenda item. The log also has value in providing evidence of the balance between the verbal contributions of appraiser and appraisee. While there can be no golden rule, one expects the greater part of the interview to be taken up by the responses of the appraisee, so that the overall proportion is at least 2:1

Observation schedule

RAPPORT
Was rapport easily and competently established by the appraiser?

How? [Examples]

Was it well maintained?

Were there occasions when it was in danger of breaking down?

Was breakdown averted? How?

QUESTIONS AND ANSWERS
Did the appraiser in general use open questions? Avoid leading questions? Avoid multiple and overcomplex questions? [Examples of good and bad practice]

At what stages were questions asked to narrow down or probe an issue?

Did the appraisee assist the process in his/her responses?

USE OF TIME
Estimate the balance between appraiser and appraisee of time spent in talking. Did it vary at different stages of the interview?

How well was the agenda covered? Was the time spent on different items appropriate? [Ask for a copy of the agenda if you do not have one]

Did the appraiser at any stage have to cut short the appraisee?

Was this done diplomatically?

FACTS AND FEELINGS
Did the appraiser summarise facts – and, if necessary, feelings – at appropriate stages of the interview?

How well did the appraiser deal with any defensive or aggressive reactions on the part of the appraisee?

Was the appraisee given the scope to represent his/her own feelings?

Were any issues skated over by either party?

DOCUMENTATION
Were the procedures for notetaking explained and accepted?

Was the recording in any way obtrusive?

Did the appraisee make notes?

Was good use made of the self-appraisal proforma?

Were the points for the contract satisfactorily reviewed at the end? [It will help if you make your own notes on items for the contract as the interview proceeds.]

and probably nearer 3:1. However, at different stages of the interview that proportion will vary considerably: at the beginning when the appraiser is concentrating on establishing rapport and at the end when she is summarising, there is likely to be a very different proportion.

Debriefing

It is our experience that most role-plays are extremely competently performed and that most observers make constructive and sympathetic observations – probably on the grounds that 'there but for the grace of God went I'! However, there will be times when the tutor has the unenviable task of handling the debriefing of a role-play that has gone wrong. In so doing, he gives, one trusts, an object lesson in achieving the greatest possible positive outcome without compromising his integrity.

A final consideration

The role-play will have been performed before an audience of up to a dozen people. Since workshops will generally have twice that number of participants, a second case study will have been prepared by another pair of groups, and there is usually a strong desire expressed to 'see both performances'. Workshop organisers must make their own decisions on this. The main disadvantages are that this will extend the programme by 90 minutes; that the audience is twice as large and therefore possibly somewhat intimidating for the role-players; that half the audience will be involved in the case study only to the extent of having had a cursory read of the initial brief; and that one pair of role-players will have had to wait on tenterhooks for their turn. Advantages lie mainly in the opportunities to compare and contrast interviewing skills and, particularly in a workshop consisting of teachers from both primary and secondary schools, to learn more about the responsibilities and management skills of the other phase.

TRAINING MATERIALS

In all the case studies which follow a first name has been chosen which is not indicative of gender, since the role-player may be of either sex and it is essential that the decision of who will role-play is left open until the last possible moment. Yet the text of the case study would be insufferably pedantic if we had striven throughout for a wording which was gender neutral: the avoidance of a 'sexist' personal pronoun – sometimes male, sometimes female, quite arbitrarily – is therefore impossible. It should be explained to workshop members that the sex of the characters is their choice, determined by the eventual selection of role-players.

In the expectation that these training materials will be used for several years, we have also avoided as far as posible any indication of the extent of experience within the case study school of appraisal interviews. Tutors may therefore decide that the appraisee is a volunteer in a school newly engaging in the introduction of appraisal or that appraisal has now become routine or even statutory. That decision will depend on both local and national circumstances.

It is advantageous if tutors intending to use a case study spend a short time, preferably collectively, identifying the strengths and weaknesses of the appraisee, of other members of staff referred to and of the institution. While the role of tutor is that of facilitator, there is much merit in being able to anticipate the issues that are likely to arise. Since this is the only experience of teacher appraisal that most staff will have before either they are appraised or they act as appraisers, it is important that the outcomes are as positive as they can be made. There will therefore be occasions when, without being overtly interventionist, the skilful tutor will nudge the simulation in a more profitable direction. Time for preparation is nearly always an issue and tutors will need to consider in advance how long any aspect of the preparation ought to take in order to ensure that it is completed on time.

Gerry Manners

Gerry Manners is curriculum coordinator for humanities in Willow Lane primary school in a prosperous commuter suburb. She has been teaching for ten years now, for the last five in this school, and is known to be contemplating applications for deputy head posts in the near future.

The primary phase adviser – who happens to be a humanities specialist – has used Gerry on a number of INSET courses and thinks highly of her. The school's headteacher had also good reason to be grateful to Gerry for undertaking certain additional duties at a time when other members of staff were, for a brief period, 'working to rule'. This action did not, however, endear Gerry to certain members of the staff, particularly the deputy head, the local secretary of a teachers' union.

The written humanities syllabus is a model of its kind and has been much used by the headteacher as an exemplar for other coordinators in the school. Its aims and objectives are clear and succinct; the year-by-year sequencing demonstrates a clear understanding of the potential for learning of pupils over the whole primary age range; and the needs of both the gifted and the slow learner have not been overlooked. The approach is pupil- and activity-centred, and each phase of the syllabus is cross-referenced to a materials and resource bank in which local 'living' resources feature prominently. Gerry devotes many hours to updating the syllabus and researching new materials.

Unfortunately the headteacher has become increasingly aware that Gerry's effectiveness as a coordinator does not appear to match up to all this excellent preparation. Except in her own class and that of a colleague who is also a close friend, most of the actual teaching tends to revert rapidly after the beginning of each term to more traditional methods, with a heavy reliance on 'chalk and talk'. Other teachers claim – with some justification – that they find themselves too preoccupied with large classes and the needs of other areas of the curriculum to devote to humanities the extensive planning that a resource-based curriculum demands. They add that what parents want – and indeed what the National Curriculum seems to be requiring – is a good solid basis of factual knowledge in history and geography, 'without frills' as one of them put it. Gerry maintains, citing the phase adviser in support, that the aims of the National Curriculum in these two subjects can be met through an integrated humanities approach.

Job specification

Curriculum coordinator for humanities: Gerry Manners

In addition to teaching his/her own class in accordance with the school curricular policy, the postholder will:

- be responsible for updating all class teachers in the content and methodology of subjects within the broad field of humanities, particularly in the light of the evolving guidelines of the National Curriculum;

- develop and maintain suitable curriculum materials and resources;

- promote the sharing by class teachers of their knowledge and experience of humanities teaching;

- explore ways of involving parents and members of the community in contributing to the humanities curriculum;

- while maintaining the required central focus on our national heritage, encourage the recognition of the part played by ethnic minorities and women, and the importance of global approaches to environmental issues;

- collaborate with other curriculum coordinators as appropriate on projects that emphasise the wholeness of human knowledge;

- communicate information about the development of the curriculum to the headteacher and deputy head;

- enlarge through in-service training his/her knowledge and skills in both the subject content and the field of education management as opportunities arise.

© Routledge 1991

Evelyn Wood

Evelyn Wood is halfway through her third year of teaching in Hawthorn Lane Primary School. She is over 30, having trained as a mature student. She has a class of thirty-four 7- to 8-year-olds.

She was regarded by her polytechnic tutors as an outstanding student, gaining consistently high grades, especially in art and drama, and was particularly commended for her final teaching practice, the highlight of which was an imaginative project on *People and Animals* which drew out first-rate work from nearly every child in the class, including some of very low ability.

During her first year at her present school it became apparent that, while her teaching was inspiring and, at times, even inspired, she showed very little organisational ability. She appeared to be having great difficulty in maintaining her records of work done or standards achieved although, to be fair to her, parents have spoken most approvingly of her knowledge of their children. The deputy head – a good manager, but one who does things 'by the book' – spoke to her a number of times in that year and, during a time when the headteacher was off ill for a lengthy period, warned her that she was very much on the borderline with regard to the satisfactory completion of her probationary period. Her record keeping, it appears, then improved dramatically. When the headteacher returned from convalescence he had a session with her in which he discovered that there were domestic difficulties. She was clearly grateful for the headteacher's personal interest and offer of support but was not willing to go into details. He has of course kept an eye on her work over the past eighteen months and, although not as censorious as the deputy appears to be, has to admit that her classroom organisation is still less than satisfactory. For example, there are always queues at her desk, orderly, because her control is good, but queues nevertheless. The children do not appear able to find apparatus for themselves and seem excessively reliant upon her, so that there is a constant stream of demands being made of her the whole day through.

Yet, when he looks at the work her children are doing in the area of the curriculum in which he himself has most expertise – language, the humanities, drama, movement, the creative arts – he has to admit that he would have been pleased to have achieved at that level in his third year of teaching. He has noticed that she often stays late, setting up displays of work which receive favourable comment from parents and other visitors. She contributes well to staff meetings, has attended in-service sessions voluntarily and is well liked by other members of staff of all ages.

It is in number work that she is undoubtedly at her weakest. The deputy, himself formerly a mathematics/science coordinator, has expressed to the headteacher concern about her standards in this area of the curriculum and the headteacher has accordingly asked the school's maths coordinator to give her as much help as possible.

This will be Evelyn's first appraisal since she became a main professional grade teacher. The headteacher has discussed her progress and shortcomings regularly with the deputy and it has been made abundantly clear that, despite the help that she is being given, her number work is still not up to the standard being achieved in the parallel age group class, as the deputy demonstrates by mean levels of achievement for the two classes plotted on a graph. The deputy also holds the view that it was time that Evelyn – now in her third year of teaching and a mature entrant to the profession at that – stood more on her own feet and made fewer demands on a very busy maths coordinator. This was made clear in a recent debriefing session after a classroom observation. Evelyn has certainly seemed decidedly troubled in the past week or so, though the headteacher suspects that this may be a consequence of some domestic upset about which she is, as usual, uncommunicative.

Although for many reasons the headteacher would like to conduct Evelyn's appraisal himself, she is in one of the years already allocated to the deputy head. It may be that Evelyn will herself bring matters to a head by seeking to exercise her right of appeal to be appraised by someone other than the deputy head. What the headteacher will do in that situation he has not yet decided.

Lee Smith

Elmley School is an 11–16 comprehensive on a housing estate, but draws from a varied social background. It is a caring school, and this reputation has been fostered by the present headteacher who has been in post for four years. It has an excellent pastoral system with well-developed schemes of personal and social education in all years, and staff carefully selected to see that pastoral care is integrated into the life of the school. It also has a good academic record, and the local tertiary college is on record as saying that the pupils from Elmley are well-balanced young adults with good learning skills.

Lee Smith has been at the school for fifteen years, as head of department for the past six. She is a highly competent and experienced teacher of modern languages, fluent in French and German and with a good working knowledge of two other languages. She makes good use of technology in her teaching, is scrupulous in her preparation and marking, and demands the highest standards of her pupils. They may grumble but they produce for her and her team some of the best GCSE results in the school.

She is a firm but unobtrusive disciplinarian. She has taken a number of school parties abroad, always with a thoroughly researched and purposive cultural and linguistic programme. Pupils know that 'you don't go for fun, you go because you want to improve your chances'. And they go.

Lee is now 46, possibly a little disenchanted by failure to achieve promotion, though she shows little sign of real ambition and is even openly critical of those who do. She is inclined to say: 'I came into the profession to teach, not to manage.' She is respected rather than liked, sociable rather than gregarious. Her hobbies are sailing and boat-building: she is a competent amateur woodworker.

The Head of Lower School, recently in post, has expressed his disappointment and concern at Lee's apparent lack of interest in her year 9 tutor group. The school has recently been much involved in fund raising for local charities, and year 9 has been in the forefront of developing community projects that are enhancing the school's reputation. 9LS has taken little part in these. When other groups are planning and discussing, or looking at social issues of importance using the study packs prepared by the Head of Lower School, 9LS is being told to get on with their homework, because 'education is about learning, not sponsored swims'. Some of the tutor group have been to see the Head of Lower School to ask if they can transfer to a 'more interesting tutor group' but so far he has not acceded to any such request. There is undoubtedly an undercurrent of discontent and frustration.

Matters came to a head recently when the Head of Lower School sought to discuss with Lee two cases of serious domestic upset concerning children in 9LS. Her response was: 'If the school wants social workers, it should employ them.'

The headteacher wondered whether a move next year to a final year tutor group might not be advantageous to all concerned and floated the suggestion with the Head of Upper School, who is, so it happens, a member of Lee's department. While not actually saying 'Over my dead body!' he made it clear that there would be considerable difficulties. 'At a personal level I think I could handle it. Unfortunately our management styles are very dissimilar. She runs departmental meetings by giving instructions – I can't remember when we last had a discussion.'

Chris Perry

For the past six years Chris Perry has been Head of Department* in the Rowan Oak comprehensive school – 11–16, sixth form entry now down to five in the lower school and declining. He had come from a similar school in a neighbouring authority. Initially progress within the department was slow. Of those staff in the department when he arrived, two were sound but traditional teachers coming up to retirement age – both rather critical and resentful of the young incomer though neither would have wanted his responsibilities. Regrettably, their influence on the department as a whole was strong and Chris found departmental discussions rather disillusioning.

Both have now gone, the first before and the second shortly after the arrival of the new headteacher just over a year ago. Their replacement – one only because of falling rolls – is experienced, competent and ready to contribute to new ideas in the department. In spite of the changed scene, a number of developments which the headteacher deems to be necessary and which were discussed with Chris nearly six months ago do not seem to have been implemented. Indeed, they *may* be in train, but Chris is by nature not very communicative and is possibly a little in awe of the new headteacher, a rather dynamic figure compared with his dull but worthy predecessor.

There is little doubt in Chris's mind that the record of this meeting will be on the agenda of the appraisal interview for which he is preparing. In addition the school's involvement in the LEA's TVEE programme is now gathering momentum, and the head will certainly want to see evidence that the department is moving smoothly into gear for this development. Relationships with the local tertiary college have in the past been patchy at best, but Chris's curriculum area is one where collaboration is highly desirable. The head can be expected to attach great weight in the appraisal interview to what Chris has achieved in developing effective liaison. Several governors have been showing considerable interest in this aspect of the school's management and the head is planning to produce a report on liaison across phases for a governors' meeting in the near future.

In this school all staff other than the head, the deputies and the music teacher are now tutors. A new teacher is, whenever possible, given at least one year to 'shadow' an experienced and able tutor and Chris has such a person, a woman much liked by all the pupils in the group. He believes that she is well able to take over his tutor group and he has suggested as much to the pastoral deputy, on the grounds that he is heavily committed with other responsibilities. The deputy was non-committal. Chris expects this matter will be raised at the appraisal interview.

NOTE
* Which department Chris is head of is left open for the appraisee group to decide. Wherever possible, a department should be chosen which would not lead any member of the group to say at an early stage: 'Well, that let's me out because I know absolutely nothing about . . .!'

The decision will determine the number of members of the department including Chris. If the subject were a core subject, English for example, being taught for 10 per cent of the timetable, then there would be a likely total of 108 periods in a 40 period week: 20 in each of years 7–9, where there are five forms, and 24 in years 10–11, where there are six. This would give an entitlement of three full-time teachers in the department, including Chris, with possibly someone from another department taking one or two classes. Using this as a guide, it should be easy for the appraisee group to work out the staffing allocation for any other department and obtain the agreement of the appraiser group.

Memorandum from Head to Chris Perry

GOALSETTING

I found this morning's meeting very helpful. I have noted down as promised a record of the areas in which you have undertaken to take action in the near future. If you have any disagreement with my record of the meeting do not hesitate to let me know.

Links with Tertiary College: contact to be made with departmental head to establish areas of common interest and concern, particularly for post-16 pupils on transfer, but also for possible TVEE collaboration next year.

Curriculum Development: plan within department for continued introduction of National Curriculum.

Curriculum Development: seek to develop interdepartmental curriculum initiatives leading to improved whole school curriculum policy. This should proceed alongside the work of the staff working party which began its discussions last month.

Appraisal: consider your role within the appraisal process for members of your department; undertake in-service training in classroom observation and appraisal interviewing.

Don't hesitate to let me or the deputy know if any difficulties arise.

Date: [six months previously]

Chapter 8

Interviewing skills

It will not have escaped the notice of readers that appraisal demands a high level of interviewing skills: active listening, appropriate questioning, negotiation and, not infrequently, counselling skills. We are well aware that time for appraisal training will be, of necessity, limited – possibly far more limited than it ought to be. We are also well aware that relatively few teachers have had training in these skills and that their acquisition is of vital importance to the success of appraisal in our LEAs and schools. We have therefore always made a point of including in our workshops a half-day session on these skills, knowing full well that we can do no more in this time than raise awareness and give some limited experience of the techniques that will be useful to appraisers and appraisees alike.

To ensure that workshop members are not led to believe that interviewing skills are somehow confined to appraisal interviews we use the value-free terms *client* and *adviser* throughout rather than appraisee and appraiser.

LISTENING SKILLS

It is essential that, even before any interview has begun, the adviser has created the conditions whereby rapport can most easily be established. Clearly there should be no interruptions: 'Where were we?', whether said or thought, destroys rapport. Other physical conditions for full attention need to be considered. The placing of chairs is important: neither in such a position that eye contact is difficult, nor placed face to face so that client and adviser are eyeballing each other. Sheaves of paper are a distraction, even a threat. If they are necessary to the interview, then a small table on which they can be put is helpful. For some people a cup of tea or coffee acts as an icebreaker. For others it may be an embarrassment: being asked a question at the very moment when you are raising the cup to your lips can be most disconcerting!

The effectiveness of the adviser can often be measured by the amount of talking he does: in general, the less he talks, the more effective the interview. Needless to say, there is no standard measurement of what the optimum extent of adviser participation is; much depends on the degree to which the client needs to be drawn out.

There should be no preconception of the way in which the client and adviser will relate. We often hear it said that two people who work closely together in a school should have no difficulty in relating well in an appraisal interview. There is no guarantee that this will be so and the adviser needs to be aware that establishing and maintaining rapport is crucial to a successful outcome. Clarification of the purpose of the interview is important; however much its purpose may seem crystal clear to the adviser, the reassurance of the client will not be time misspent.

Many years ago, in a leaflet on interviewing prepared for the Civil Service, we came upon the helpful aphorism: 'An interview is a conversation with a purpose.' One of the tasks of the adviser is to keep the conversation to its purpose. There are times when considerable judgment is required to know whether what is being said is unconsciously – or possibly even consciously – creating a diversion from the main purpose. That diversion may be important to the client and should not be lightly disregarded. Nevertheless, there are times when it should be identified openly as a distraction from the interview and an undertaking given that time will be found for discussion of that issue on another occasion. Peters and Waterman (1982) in *In Search of Excellence* have the happy phrase: 'Stick to the knitting.'

There is an ongoing need for the adviser to reassure the client that he has heard and understood what has been said to him. This is done in two ways: by verbal and non-verbal signals; and by reflecting data and feelings. The verbal signals are often scarcely words at all, rather murmurs of encouragement and agreement; the non-verbal signals are nods and smiles and, above all, a body language that signifies full attention and empathy. It is not being suggested that the adviser will consciously seek to introduce these signals. They come as part of the normal behaviour of most good listeners. It is, however, helpful to remind advisers that these signals have a powerful effect on the establishing of rapport.

Reflecting data is a more overt technique. This is a specific contribution to the dialogue from the adviser which says, in effect: 'I believe I have understood you to make this point.' If the adviser has accurately summarised what the client has been saying this has a twofold effect: first of reassurance, and secondly of encouraging the client either to elaborate further or to move to a new aspect of the matter under discussion. If the adviser has been mistaken in his understanding, the client has the opportunity to correct the misapprehension. It is unimportant whether the misconception has come from the client's misrepresentation or the adviser's faulty perception: there is no merit in apportioning blame. An anxious client may well be unnecessarily iterative, and reflecting data is a means of moving the dialogue on to new ground without appearing to be impatient.

Reflecting feelings is no less important. Here the skilled adviser perceives what lies behind the words: personal anxieties, concerns about what is professionally proper to raise in the interview, self-doubts, something being hidden and so on. It is a matter of judgment on the part of the adviser as to whether these should be brought to the surface at this stage of the dialogue or even at all. There are no criteria by which one can advise on this. However, if there is a general climate of open behaviour in the institution, it can reasonably be assumed that self-disclosure can and should be encouraged.

There are occasions when the adviser may feel the need to go a little further than merely reflecting data or feelings. It may be necessary to find out what lies behind a client's words or to draw together what appears to have been implied in a number of different statements. The skill of interpreting is one of the most difficult for the adviser, since it is essential for him to avoid making judgments or to put words into the mouth of the client. To keep the interpretation open, that is to give the client the freedom to say 'That is not at all what I was saying', it is necessary to cast the interpretation in the form of a question: 'Is this what you mean?'; or alternatively to preface a statement with the words 'If I understand you correctly . . .'.

The way in which questions are framed by the adviser is of considerable importance. They should be purposive and simple. Complex, and particularly multiple questions, can be very disconcerting to the client. They add to the tension that he is already likely to be feeling and consequently set up a need for rapport to be re-established. They should also be focused primarily on the needs of the client. Appraisal interviews must not become an opportunity for the adviser to score points. It is vital that what the client contributes to the dialogue is properly recognised; and, no less important, that what he is as a person is fully valued. Aggressive behaviour on the part of the adviser will soon create a barrier of mistrust. The client is likely to begin covertly to question the true purpose of the dialogue and to set up further barriers himself.

Yet no dialogue should be allowed to become cosy: this helps neither party. Confrontation is not of itself a bad behaviour. It only becomes so when rapport is lost and the client no longer sees the value of open behaviour. It should be used with caution. To highlight inconsistencies can be destructive and demoralising or positive and appreciated, depending entirely on the skill with which they are presented. Probes similarly can either puncture the self-esteem of the client or nudge him towards a greater self-perception. It is of crucial importance for the adviser not to store up issues and later to confront the client with them: inconsistencies should be identified as they occur and every attempt made to enable the client to perceive them for himself.

Unmasking is a behaviour that must be used with the utmost discretion. By this we mean revealing to the client that he is deluding himself or that there is clear evidence that what he has been saying does not square up with the facts. There are times when it will have to be done; it can be a traumatic experience but it can also be a cathartic one if well handled.

Advice and information should come almost wholly at the request of the client. The adviser will lose ground if he imposes his views of what is to be done on the client. At the same time it should be recognised that a skilful adviser can, without manipulation, encourage the client to seek advice or information.

BUILDING FOR FUTURE ACTION

In working towards any kind of action plan with a client, the adviser now has other considerations to bear in mind: the relationship with the departmental or the whole school policy of what is now being discussed and will eventually be agreed as the desired new state. In goalsetting, for example, the role of the adviser is somewhat more proactive and therefore calls for other, additional skills.

It is helpful to have in mind the first three stages of Management by Objectives:

- Where are you now?
- Where do you want to get to?
- How will you get there?

The first stage may seem self-evident, but for the hard-pressed teacher, for whom the grindstone is so obtrusive that he can see no further than his nose, some time for reflection on his present situation is important. Without a clear and precise analysis of the present situation, it is impossible to consider the appropriate path to a desired future state.

However, the movement from the first to the second stage is not to be thought of as wholly linear. In order to identify realisable goals, it is first necessary for the adviser to encourage the client to identify the full range of options that are open to him. Sometimes this can be done in a brainstorming session: although the list of options may look formidable by the end, the speed with which ideas have been proposed precludes the making of judgments. The sorting process — 'making sense of the storm' — makes the list less formidable as patterns emerge.

In order to select from a list of options those which are more viable, it is necessary for the client and adviser to agree the criteria whereby that choice may be made. Some of these criteria may lie outside the decision-making parameters of both client and adviser; in such a situation advice from those who have the ability to decide must be obtained in order that the criteria may be wholly appropriate to the diagnostic process. What is important,

Figure 8.1 Listening skills

The good listener . . .

■ gives the greater part of any interview to:

Drawing out

This requires:

- full attention
- no haste, but an eye on the purpose
- the regular testing of understanding
- the encouragement of self-disclosure
- questions that are:

  ▲ client-centred
  ▲ open
  ▲ clearly phrased
  ▲ purposive

■ gives a substantial part of any interview to:

Supporting

This requires:

- the recognition of the client's value
- evidence of care and concern
- an atmosphere of mutual trust

■ gives some time to

Confronting

This requires:

- open behaviour
- direct feedback
- the highlighting of inconsistencies
- careful probing

and *very occasionally*

- unmasking

■ gives the least time to:

Advising and **informing**

© Routledge 1991

however, is that reference to a higher authority should not be seen by the client as taking the decision out of his hands. What is being sought is not a ruling but information which will enable an effective and viable decision to be made.

It follows, then, that as far as possible the identification of options and of the criteria which will be used to validate and select from these options rests in the ownership of the client. The adviser can only increase the client's readiness and capacity for change; he cannot bring about that change. The client must own the change process. Nevertheless it often happens that the client wants instant solutions and therefore identifies only the most obvious options. It is an important part of the adviser's role to generate alternatives until both client and adviser can be sure that they have the full range of options before them for the selection of goals or the devising of an action plan.

One well-tried and effective strategy for testing what has now become, after this selection, a desired goal or plan is force-field analysis (Lewin, 1947) as illustrated in Figure 8.2. The centre line in the diagram is the present state, representing the answer to the question: where are you now? The goal at the top is the desired state, representing the proposed answer to the question: where do you want to get to? *Forces for* are those supportive factors which either currently exist or which can be brought into play and which will promote the movement towards the desired state; *forces against* are the restraining factors which will inhibit the movement towards the desired state. An assessment is now made of the strength of these forces, either by the length of arrows towards the goal for the supportive factors and away for the restraining factors, or by coding them L, M and H for low, medium and high.

When all the possible positive and negative forces have been entered on the diagram, two questions are now asked and applied to each entry:

- what can be done to enhance the forces for the achievement of the goal?
- what can be done to minimise the forces against the achievement of the goal?

It is easy for the client to be self-deluding here, either by being excessively optimistic about the possibility of raising positive forces or by laying too much emphasis on the negative forces. Inevitably, the process is highly subjective. There is therefore an important role for the adviser in encouraging the client to a balanced judgment. It is here that he will deploy a valuable skill, that of building vision by encouraging the client to envisage both a desired future state and the means of getting there.

However, force-field analysis is a good analytical tool only if it is used with a sense of realism. It may well help the client to answer the question: how will you get there? It may also provide the answer to another question, no less important: are you sure that 'there' is where you wanted to get to?

Figure 8.2 Force-field analysis

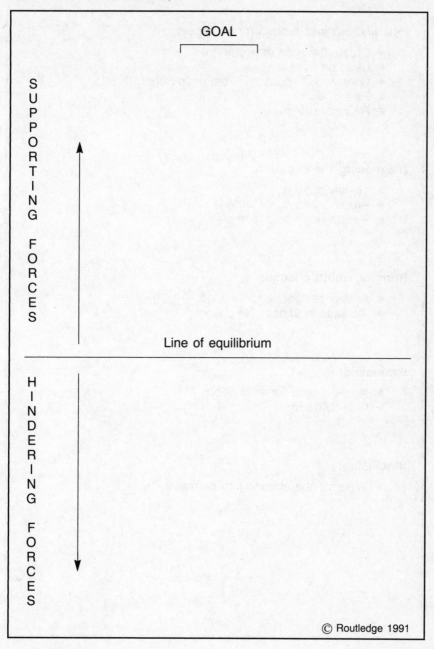

Figure 8.3 Key stages in the interviewing process

Establishing and maintaining rapport:

- Create the right environment
- Keep on course
- Give verbal and non-verbal encouragement
- Reflect data
- Reflect feelings

Diagnosing the situation:

- Identify options
- Propose and agree criteria
- Decide goals or action plan

Bringing about change:

- Assess readiness for change
- Increase readiness for change

Evaluating:

- Agree criteria for evaluation
- Plan follow-up

Stabilising:

- Integrate the change into normal behaviour

© Routledge 1991

Sometimes the outcome of the exercise is to demonstrate that the goal is unattainable, either totally or as it now stands. In the latter case, there will be clear indications of the ways in which it can be modified to make it realisable.

A summary of the key stages in the interviewing process appears in Figure 8.3. This is particularly useful when taken in conjunction with the triad training exercise which follows in the next section.

TRAINING FOR INTERVIEWING SKILLS

One of the most effective forms of training is through triads. This requires sufficient space to enable workshop members to group themselves in threes so that discussion in one triad does not impinge upon that in another. Beyond that, it requires little planning. Even those workshop members who, having received the handout on page 148, have sometimes been overheard to say 'I have no idea what issue I can possibly bring to my triad' are almost always next seen to be in full spate!

As trainers we always advise workshop members that we are available if wanted but that we will not otherwise sit in on a triad. This is for two reasons. The first is that our presence adds an unnecessary dimension to the group and almost certainly detracts from the important learning process for the observer, since we are often looked to for comments which he should be offering. Indeed, it is sometimes not perceived that the observer is required to exercise the same interviewing skills in his debriefing as the adviser in his dialogue with the client. The second reason is that, were we to move from one group to another, we would find it virtually impossible to judge the timing of our arrival to coincide with the beginning of the second or third round; and to arrive after the start would be disconcerting to all parties.

It is important that, in training, the interview is brought to a conclusion before any decisions are made about what the change process should be. This is because the adviser is not in a position to take responsibility for the stages which follow.

One lighthearted exercise which takes no more than half an hour at most is the quiz which concludes this section. In part it provides examples of some of the listening skills referred to earlier in this chapter and thus reinforces understanding of skills such as *reflecting feelings* or *probing*. It illustrates behaviours which are unhelpful, like *reminiscing*, or positively harmful, like *taking over ownership* and *judging*. One, in particular, *diverting*, is ambivalent and depends on the circumstances. It may be used in a positive way to ease the client back on to the main line when he has gone down an unproductive sidetrack; but, thoughtlessly used, it may prove to be riding roughshod over the client's perceptions of his needs in the dialogue. Several behaviours may seem interchangeable but do in fact have nuances of differentiation which it is worth exploring: *clarifying* and *reflecting data*, for example.

Working in triads

Each member of the triad in turn takes the role of client, adviser and observer.

As *client*, think of a professional situation concerning which you would welcome advice. The situation may be one that you are having to address in the near future; or it may be one that you are already engaged in but which appears likely to have further stages of development.

As *adviser*, your main task is to create an atmosphere in which the client will speak freely, and will seek and value your help in the diagnosis of the situation. In training, establishing rapport usually presents no problem; but you do need to be aware of its importance both at the beginning and throughout the dialogue and to be alert to all opportunities for making the client feel at ease.

As *observer*, your role is to comment and, particularly, promote discussion on the adviser's role concept, influencing skills and interviewing techniques. These include:

- active listening

- empathising

- appropriate questioning

- defining and clarifying the issue

NOTE: It is sometimes necessary in training for the observer to intervene to indicate that the interview now appears to have gone beyond the state of diagnosing the situation and is entering that of bringing about change. No other intervention should be needed.

If there is time, the triad should seek to draw some conclusions about the expertise required for any of the skills listed above or for others that they have identified as a result of the exercise.

Active listening

Here is a list of typical observations made by interviewers. Not all are examples of good practice!

1 Link each with its appropriate keyword from the list below.
2 Tick the box to indicate those listening skills you regard as the most important/positive.
3 Mark with a cross any you regard as particularly unhelpful – or positively harmful!

[CA] CAPPING	[CL] CLARIFYING	[D] DIVERTING
[E] EMPATHISING	[I] INVITING	[J] JUDGING
[L] LEAVING A WAY OUT	[OD] OPENING DOORS	[P] PROBING
[RD] REFLECTING DATA	[RF] REFLECTING FEELINGS	[RM] REMINISCING
	[T] TAKING OVER OWNERSHIP	

Would you rather we took this up on another occasion?   □

Yes, you are right. The overcrowding does create problems . . .   □

I don't think I have quite understood. Which class did you say?   □

Is that really so? You have spoken to . . . and there has been no change? Could you let me have more details?   □

When I was a class teacher in the Sixties . . .   □

You say it was a disastrous lesson. Would you like to talk about it?   □

In that situation you made a totally wrong decision.   □

I must say I share your worries about . . .   □

Yes, your classroom *is* overcrowded. I have put this matter on the agenda of the next staff meeting. Now tell me about the newspaper project.   □

I think you have touched on something important there. What was your reaction?   □

Are other staff as concerned about this issue as you are?   □

You don't want to worry about that! I'll sort it out for you.   □

If you think you have too much to do, then all I can say is that you ought to see the amount of work I take home every evening!   □

Chapter 9

Management performance

As we have indicated in Chapter 2, in every secondary school and in a majority of primary schools there will be assistant teachers whose appraisal, if based primarily on classroom performance, would not justly reflect their skills and responsibilities. It is arguable, of course, that every teacher is also a manager and it is true that some element of managerial performance will form part of every appraisal interview. However, what we have in mind here are those teachers – deputy heads and those with major curricular, pastoral or sectional responsibility – whose performance within these responsibilities significantly influences the managerial standing of the school as an institution. We do not think it appropriate for us, as trainers, to be more precise in prescribing those for whom specific appraisal of managerial performance is needed. The decision is one to be made within a LEA or more probably by the school itself.

We are concerned that there is already evident a marked tendency towards the promotion of a top-down model of appraisal of managerial performance, both because it will be administratively convenient and because, in spite of a trend towards more corporate styles of management, a majority of schools are still hierarchically structured and managed. Thus, in many secondary schools, it will still be the function of the curriculum deputy to comment on the managerial skill of heads of departments, and of the pastoral deputy to comment on that of heads of school, year or house. In all but the largest primary schools the responsibility for management was once the sole prerogative of the headteacher. As managerial responsibilities have multiplied, we have in recent years seen the devolution of some major areas of management from the headteacher to the deputy head and, often, the head of early years. While in both secondary and primary schools the perspective of these senior postholders is undoubtedly important, they may well, it needs to be recognised, have a somewhat one-sided view of the managerial performance of other staff. There is clearly a need for a bivalent approach to the appraisal of middle managers.

We do not find ourselves attracted to the contention that:

so far as subject specialist coordinators in primary schools and heads of department in secondary schools are concerned there is clearly a role for local authority advisers and inspectors.

(Wragg, 1987)

Advisory staff in all authorities are already overworked and are likely to be even more stretched if they are to be involved in the appraisal of headteachers as proposed in the document *School Teacher Appraisal: A National Framework* (HMSO, 1989). The appointment of more advisory teachers for this purpose, 'possibly on a three-year assignment, and for them to undertake such work on a regular basis', as Wragg also suggests, seems impracticable in the light of LMS, since the cost of these appointments will almost certainly have to be found by 'claw-back' from schools' budgets and is not likely to be acceptable to headteachers or governing bodies.

It is generally accepted that curriculum advisers will, from their contact with heads of department and curriculum coordinators outside the context of the school, have a contribution to make to the data collection for the appraisal of these postholders. It is also true that phase and general advisers will frequently be able to offer valuable perceptions about the managerial performance of deputies and other senior managers. However, we believe that there is no need to go outside the school for the actual appraisal of middle and senior managers; indeed, we think that there is positive harm in so doing, since there is every likelihood of a shift, consciously or unconsciously, from the formative to the summative if this were to become policy. What is needed in order that the view may be comprehensive and balanced is something that takes us further into the structure of the school, not away from it. We would strongly recommend the inclusion of an element of peer group appraisal.

Peer group appraisal is a much misunderstood term. In *Appraising Teachers in Schools* (Bell, 1988) Norman Thomas, admittedly writing particularly of primary schools in which he has a wealth of experience, refers to the 'senior/junior relationship between appraiser and appraisee'. We would argue that this hierarchical relationship, while by no means superseded by other forms of managerial relationships, is becoming increasingly inappropriate and even a barrier to effective management, in both secondary and primary schools. Mintzberg (1979) classifies a school as a 'professional bureaucracy' regarding it as:

a decentralised structure in which the classroom teachers . . . seek to exert collective control over the administrative decisions which affect them. Coordination is therefore by mutual adjustment, a democratic process, with liaison devices in the middle line management.

(Dennison and Shenton, 1987)

It is clear from an examination of the organisational tree of most secondary schools that there are parallel hierarchies in which the subordinate in one may be the superordinate in another. A head of department may serve as form tutor responsible to a senior pastoral manager who will be a classroom teacher within his or another department. A headteacher or deputy may have a teaching commitment within a department and regard herself – and genuinely be regarded by other members – as subordinate to the head of that department. Within primary schools, where holders of incentive allowances and main professional grade teachers alike have managerial responsibilities for areas of the curriculum, status based on salary is becoming meaningless.

Our contention, therefore, is that while there are hierarchies within schools, both those which derive from the stratification of salary scale, seniority and level of responsibility and those which stem from custom, these do not necessarily equate with line management. There are many circumstances in which the concept of senior and junior, superordinate and subordinate, may be profoundly misleading. Furthermore, there is a very real need for a clear understanding of the level of performance of a manager not solely from the perspective of those to whom he may be responsible but also from that of those for whom he has responsibility.

There is a fear, by no means without foundation, among many teachers that appraisal will accentuate the traditional hierarchies that lie not too deeply hidden beneath what to them is the more acceptable progression towards corporate management. Trethowan (1987), for example, states categorically that '[the] problem of multiple accountability is best tackled by the line and project approach'. This he demonstrates by the case study of a language teacher who has a tutor group and a responsibility for coaching a sports team. Indeed, it may well be the case here that the Head of the Languages Department *is* the appraiser to whom the Year Head and Head of PE contribute 'feedback', to use his terminology. However, we do not think that this case study truly represents the issue we are seeking to identify. We are concerned with the concept of mutuality which we believe should underpin the management of our schools and therefore the appraisal of all who manage in them.

We hold, and have argued repeatedly, that every appraisal *by* an appraiser is also an appraisal *of* the appraiser: that is, that the process is reciprocal and needs to be recognised as that if the organisation is to thrive. We therefore see no reason why a secondary head of department, for example, should not, during her appraisal interviews with members of her department, ascertain their views of her style of leadership, ability to communicate and other managerial skills, and then to bring those views openly to her own appraisal interview. Indeed, we would go further and argue that she might at an appropriate departmental meeting seek out the collective views of her team, preferably handing over the chair to another member of staff. By so doing she would not appear to be in a position of authority and, furthermore, would be better placed to listen more and respond less. We see the same principles governing the relationship in a primary school between, for example, the head of early years and her staff.

There are those who see peer group involvement only as a dilution or corruption of the appraisal process. Indeed Trethowan (1987) goes on to argue that an appraiser 'who, to secure a good performance rating had only to impress his or her staff, may not direct his or her decisions for the good of the organisation but rather for the gratification of the staff'. This seems to question the integrity of the teaching profession and, in its use of the term 'performance rating', at the same time demonstrates a preoccupation with appraisal as a summative rather than a formative process.

We see peer group involvement in the assessment of managerial performance as best considered through the metaphor of the mirror in which the manager is enabled to see himself. The proforma on pages 152–3 has a dual purpose. It is a means of enabling the manager to make a personal assessment of strengths and weaknesses. At the same time it can be used as a framework whereby members of a department, for example, may organise their thoughts individually or collectively about the performance standards of their head of department; or curriculum coordinators that of the primary school deputy head. It is emphatically not intended to be judgmental. We envisage the proforma being used mainly within a department, a year group, a curriculum committee, a working party or any such group within the school's management structure as a basis for open discussion. Whether or not the discussion should be chaired by the person who will later appraise the manager is a decision for the group or the school to make. The discussion should be seeking a consensus view, both among the members of the group and between the manager and those within the group. A dissentient voice among the group membership may well indicate to the manager someone who needs help. A significant difference at any point between the self-perception and the group perception indicates an area that should, in the interest of good managerial relationships, be given serious consideration by the manager.

Since for a high proportion of teachers the appraisal of managerial performance is a significant element of the formal appraisal interview, it is plainly helpful if these perceptions can be brought into the field of discussion. One useful strategy will be for the manager as appraisee to complete the proforma anew, collating his own views of his performance with those of his group and to provide this as documentation in preparation for the interview. Often the differences between the self-perception and that of the group will be negligible, and a gloss on the manager's own proforma is all that is needed. If, however, the appraiser has been involved in the role of chair of the group discussion, then she will probably have a clear view of any divergent opinions and is well placed to discuss these with

Appraising management performance

Below you will find a number of areas in which the performance of a teacher as manager may be considered. Indications of what might lie within this area are included, but these are not intended to be comprehensive. Make notes on your performance/ that of your colleague under the following general headings:

COMMUNICATING
Passing on information – filtering out necessary from unnecessary information – updating – obtaining information when requested.

RECORDING
Minute taking and dissemination – noting decisions accurately.

DECISION-MAKING
Sharing data – openness to opinions of others – reflecting consensus to superiors/subordinates – dealing with major differences – decisiveness.

PLANNING
Establishment of sound structures – differentiation between long-term, medium-term and short-term objectives – encouragement of stability – capacity to manage crises.

LEADERSHIP
Acceptance of responsibility – participative style – clear definition of goals and tasks – good relationships – supportive behaviours – power used to good effect.

MOTIVATION
Setting of good example – creation of sense of belonging to organisation – recognition of personal worth of others – recognition of strengths and limitations of others.

EDUCATIONAL PHILOSOPHY
Clear concepts – conveyance of values and beliefs to others.

PERSONAL QUALITIES

the appraisee. A further possibility is that the appraiser, if she has not been involved, uses the same proforma to make her preliminary assessment of the manager's performance and shares this with the appraisee. An exchange of proformas before any formal meeting may well highlight for both parties those divergent areas where discussion will be most fruitful and those where there is already common understanding.

It is through strategies such as this that the staff development element of appraisal can best be promoted. When staff see that serious consideration is being given to their involvement in the process, there is every reason to expect that the outcomes will be, not fractious, but beneficial to the management of the institution as a whole.

TRAINING FOR APPRAISING MANAGERIAL PERFORMANCE

Peer appraisal

Where appraisal training is school-based, there is considerable merit in trialling peer group appraisal of managerial performance. This requires a volunteer group of staff: a secondary school department or pastoral team; a primary school curriculum coordinator and a representative group of staff; a senior management team in either phase.

The trialling is in three stages as shown on the facing page. Copies of the management performance proforma on pages 152–3 will be required.

Trialling peer group appraisal of managers

STAGE I

Before the session the proforma is completed, by the team on the manager being appraised, and by the manager. What you write will not be seen by anyone other than yourself, but your contribution to discussion will be improved by this preparation.

STAGE II

Decide in advance whether you want a neutral chairperson or whether the chair can be taken by a member of the team. The views of the team are discussed heading by heading. As far as possible reach a consensus view. The manager may respond at any time, but may prefer to wait until the views of the team have been heard, either heading by heading, or entirely.

STAGE III

The trainer has attended as observer of the *process*. The final session is a debriefing by the trainer on the effectiveness of the trial. This may lead to a report back to the staff as a whole for a decision on whether or not peer group appraisal for managers should be built into the appraisal process and, if so, at what level of seniority.

Management case study

This case study is intended as a basis for discussion of how, through the appraisal process, a headteacher might move a deputy towards a more managerial role. It is designed to highlight the relationship between personal management styles and the needs of the institution, and the effectiveness of the appraisal process in seeking to reconcile them.

CEDARS ROAD PRIMARY SCHOOL

This school is well regarded by the parents in the neighbourhood and maintains a steady enrolment year by year. It has been successful academically, has a good record in sporting and cultural activities, is a caring institution and has had no difficulty in obtaining and keeping staff. Nevertheless Margaret Allanby, the new headteacher, in post a year, is concerned that the school may well not be achieving its true potential. The previous headteacher, a woman of considerable experience, had run the school as a benevolent dictatorship and was within a few years of retirement when illness cut short her career. Edgar Davey, her deputy, had ably kept the ship afloat during the headteacher's illness and as acting head after her resignation, but was not an applicant for the headship. There is a marked difference in their perceptions of their respective management roles, which you will doubtless be able to detect by being privy to their musings which follow.

Margaret Allanby, Headteacher

Nearly at the end of my first year here. In spite of the many responsibilities of a first headship, I have enjoyed it much more than I expected. It is a competent school that has the potential to respond well to the challenge of change, though I think it could easily begin on a downward spiral if I am not vigilant. Coming from a school where staff participated freely in discussion and decision-making, I was a little taken aback to find everyone looking to me for the answers.

I had been so sure that Edgar would be antagonistic – after all, he had been acting head for almost a year, and I am nearly ten years younger. As it turned out he couldn't have been more cooperative, in his own way, that is. Doors are opened, chairs offered, books carried, and he sorts out all the day-to-day staff problems for me. Sometimes, though, I do wonder if the staff are really quite as contented as he seems to think they are.

I was surprised at first that he had not applied for the headship, though he is still young enough to have done so. I think I am beginning to understand why. He does have a very limited view of his own competency. Or, to be more precise, of what his own job specification should be. Not that he would ever have used that phrase. He was quite taken aback a few weeks ago when I put to him certain ideas about what areas of management he might be interested in undertaking as from the new school year.

He became very uptight when I outlined a role vis à vis staff development. He sees himself as keeping them up to the mark in record keeping, punctuality and so on, but not for the world would he venture to make any suggestions about methodology. 'Mrs Allanby', – never Margaret, even though I use his first name in the office – 'they're professionals!' he said. In his book the classroom is the teacher's kingdom, and he would only enter it if he had to quell a riot, a most unlikely event in Cedars! Yet I have to acknowledge that he does have a pretty fair idea of what is going on in the classrooms, and school discipline is first-rate.

I wish I could persuade him to take a wider perspective of his job. Writing the job specification was one thing; winning him heart and mind for it is quite another. I can't reach him through ambition, but equally I can't have him staying here as he is for the next ten years or so.

Where can I begin? No point in sending him on a management course. Even if I did he would probably find some good reason for backing down at the last moment. I can't get him to take the chair for staff meetings, as I did when I was a deputy. I learnt the other day that all the time he was acting head he never held a staff meeting other than to pass on information or instructions. Working with parents? Liaison with the secondary school? LFM?

Well, I am determined that all staff shall have job specifications drawn up over the next six months in preparation for appraisal and I feel I must begin at the top. I have done mine and intend to share it with staff shortly and I want to do the same with Edgar's. So here goes!

Job specification: Deputy Head

To be responsible for:

- the teaching of his own class in collaboration with a 40 per cent part-time teacher. The approach to learning will be through active pupil involvement and the deputy head will be responsible for ensuring that his assistant's methodology accords with his own and with overall school policy;

- ensuring that pupil dress and behaviour is in accordance with the school policy as approved by governors;

- ensuring that staff are punctual in their attendance and punctilious in the preparation of lessons;

- cover arrangements for absent staff;

- making suitable arrangements for assemblies, so that responsibility is devolved to class teachers at least twice a week, thus ensuring full pupil participation;

- coordinating the work of curriculum coordinators so that there is a coherent understanding by all staff of the content and methodologies appropriate to the attainment targets of the National Curriculum;

- arranging parents' consultation evenings and developing strategies for keeping parents well informed of the school's aims and practices.

Edgar Davey, deputy head

I cannot make out what Mrs Allanby expects of me. I have been doing this job for over twelve years as efficiently as I know how. Parents, governors and staff have often congratulated me on my part in running a tight ship. The discipline in this school is good. The staff are happy, or at least as happy as any teachers can be in this time of rapid change. Certainly I don't hear that defeatist talk that I believe is abroad in so many staff rooms these days. Why then does she want me to interfere when everything seems to be so satisfactory? My job is surely to see to the day-to-day running of the school, not to be responsible for staff training.

She's a thoroughly nice person. I was, I have to admit, a little concerned at first about whether I would get on well with her. After all, I served under her predecessor for a long while and I wasn't looking forward to change at my time of life. I am sure Mrs Allanby means well. Just a little over-enthusiastic, I suppose. No doubt she'll settle down when she gets used to our ways. Stability is what this school needs. I pride myself on having kept it on an even keel last year in what could have been a very awkward time.

I do hope she is not going to make this appraisal business an excuse for pushing more and more management jobs on to me. If I had wanted to be a manager, I dare say I would have applied for the post of head last year. Still she has made it clear that appraisal is a two-way business, so perhaps this is my opportunity to convince her that while some of these ideas are all very well in theory – and even in practice perhaps in less fraught times – our main task these days is to demonstrate that the school is in good heart and continuing to establish the groundwork on which our young people will be able to build as they move on to secondary school.

Chapter 10

Headteacher appraisal

When in 1985 one of Somerset's most experienced headteachers was seconded to Bristol University for two terms to make an in-depth study of appraisal for that LEA, his remit was to look into secondary headteacher appraisal: 'secondary' both because this was his own area of experience and because the comparatively few secondary schools in the LEA made a detailed survey of practice and opinion feasible; and 'headteacher' on the grounds that, if the appraisal process of the leading manager of the school can be got right, that of other members of staff should follow with relative ease. *Secondary Headteacher Appraisal: The Nub of Credibility* (Gane, 1986) is a well-researched and cogently argued investigation, and undoubtedly contributed much to the choice of that authority as one of the six pilot schemes.

To say that headteachers had in the past been given little indication by their LEAs of the criteria under which they might be appraised is an understatement of some magnitude. Morgan *et al.* (1983) had in their research into secondary headteacher selection, the POST project as it became known, found 'only one of 85 LEAs which . . . provided a written description of its view of the full range of secondary heads' duties'. They too, as we have done in Chapter 6, differentiated between generic and specific elements in the job descriptions, but found no instance of selectors using these elements to identify the requirements for a particular post. Two years later the same team, now completing a follow-up study on the role of the secondary headteacher, concluded that 'a satisfactory definition of headship must include how heads approach the job as well as the tasks they perform' (Hall *et al.*, 1985).

APPRAISING AGAINST WHAT CRITERIA?

If it is important for the appraisal of assistant teachers that they have a clear concept of goals agreed with their managers and consonant with whole school policy, then surely it is no less important that headteachers have the same clarity about *their* goals. Indeed, since their goals are very much the determinants of that whole school policy, unless there is that clarity how can the performance of other teachers within the school be properly appraised? This question in its turn raises another crucial issue: with whom will headteachers clarify their goals?

Increasingly the weight of administrative and managerial responsibility is leading many headteachers, particularly of secondary schools and large primary schools, towards corporate or collegial management. The senior management team is no longer, as it was once in many schools, a convenient shorthand form for the headteacher, the deputies and possibly one or two other senior members of staff, but without any clear definition of the team's function. It is now coming to mean a group of senior staff who not only share with the headteacher the decision-making but also severally assume responsibility for particular areas of management. Readers will not need to be reminded that the ultimate responsibility rests with the headteacher; but, the more the school is charged with complex and innovatory task networks, the more delegation *with authority to act* becomes the necessary mode. Implementing and monitoring the introduction of the National Curriculum, for example, may in a primary school become part of the job specification of the deputy head, working according to guidelines planned with the headteacher. Undertaking the budgetary control required by the introduction of Local Financial Management may similarly become the province of a senior teacher in a secondary school.

In the mid-1970s, Meredydd Hughes contributed a chapter entitled 'The professional-as-administrator: the case of the secondary school head' to a symposium edited by Peters (1976). In it he sought, on the evidence of an extensive research project, first to differentiate between two models of headship, the head as chief executive and the head as leading professional, and secondly to reconcile and unify the two models. It is now patently obvious that 'the specialised work of maintaining the organisation in operation' (Barnard, 1938) can no longer be reserved to the headteacher as chief executive, but must be shared if headteachers are to survive. Even more to the point, if one accepts the contention by Hughes that 'the chief executive is concerned both with what happens within the organisation *and with the relation of the organisation to the wider system of which it is part*' [our italics], the increasing contact between individual members of the senior staff of schools and officers and advisers of the LEA of itself leads to a corporate concept of the chief executive role.

In his attempt to reconcile the chief executive role with the leading professional role, Hughes draws a distinction between the traditional and innovative aspects of a headteacher's professionalism, and concludes 'an innovating emphasis is more easily reconciled with the head's managerial responsibilities'. Today few educationists would talk about the 'traditional', but rather would differentiate between the maintenance and innovative functions of leadership. The message here is surely that, if all the members of the collegial team are successfully to combine the chief executive and the leading professional roles, they must each have within their job specifications goals which are concerned with maintenance and with innovation. Needless to say, this applies also to the headteacher.

If it is accepted that headteachers' successful management of their schools will be heavily dependent on the achievements, at all levels, of their staff, it would seem to follow that their appraisal ought to focus largely on the processes of management rather than the quantifiable outcomes. Much energy is currently being expended on seeking to set up batteries of performance indicators whereby one school can be measured against another. Accountability is, of course, the vogue word for the new decade; but it may well be that the expenditure of energy and ingenuity in seeking measurements of 'throughputs' and 'outputs' will in the long run prove to be counterproductive to sound educational management. The appraisal of headteachers ought primarily to be concerned with the extent to which, on the one hand, they have facilitated, inspired, planned, evaluated and stabilised within the school; and, on the other hand, sought and achieved for the school a public image as a caring centre of learning. It is not easy to find measuring rods which will quantify achievements in these domains.

APPRAISING HEADTEACHERS

In one respect the role of headteachers is unique: however much they may have shared or devolved responsibility, they are the members of staff who are wholly accountable to their governing bodies and their LEAs for what goes on in their schools. Their appraisal must therefore look inward, to the success of their leadership of the school, and outward to the success of their relations with governors, LEAs and the public and their implementation of local and national policy. Not surprising, then, is the following recommendation (para 19) by the National Steering Group (DES, 1989a):

> The pilot projects have demonstrated the advantages of arrangements in which headteachers are appraised by two appraisers. The additional appraiser adds a valuable further perspective on the complex job of the head and can assist in the task of collecting data for the appraisal.

The draft National Framework (DES 1990b) specifies that 'one of the two appraisers should be an officer of the LEA' and that 'where one appraiser is expected to play a larger role than the other' that person should have 'experience as a headteacher relevant to conditions in the phase in which the appraisee head works'.

There are two ways in which an LEA can nominate the peer group appraiser: it can identify from among its practising primary and secondary headteachers a number who will be offered secondment for a given period to act as headteacher appraisers; or it can identify a considerably larger number who will continue in post but be allowed extra staffing to compensate for the time that they will be engaged in appraisal activities. For this latter group, the NSG report recommends that a serving head-teacher 'should not be involved in the appraisal programme of more than three other headteachers at any one time' (para 23).

The former proposal has the advantage that, as experience in this role grows, so will the expertise. This superintendent model, as it is generally described, was wholeheartedly commended by Graham in *Those Having Torches* (Suffolk LEA, 1985): 'We would . . . assert quite definitely that the "promotion" of experienced headteachers to fill this role [of area superintendents] is the only acceptable and logical way forward.' Later, in his contribution to the DES appraisal conference (DES, 1986), Graham waxed even more lyrical:

> I predict that we will find that a new breed of animal will emerge – from the ranks of heads, advisers, teachers, officers – those with a particular expertise in an exacting craft, and that they will conduct assessment of senior staff, and supervise the wider process within schools and in partnership with heads.

This 'new breed of animal' has clearly not found favour with the NSG or with the teaching profession at large. Even the phrase 'in partnership' does little to ease the disquiet that 'conduct assessment' and 'supervise the . . . process' give rise to.

Nevertheless, the rejection of the concept of superperson-appraiser does not of itself rule out the concept of seconded headteachers. An obvious disadvantage lies in the fact that those selected for this role might well be seen by their peers as increasingly losing touch with the day-to-day realities of running a school, such is the rate of change in education today. There are problems too for the LEA in selecting the secondees. The highly successful headteacher may not be as enamoured as some might think with the prospect of being seconded for, say, a three-year stint. Some headteachers well known to us who were seconded to regional posts in the heyday of TVEI, for example, found re-entry to their former posts not without attendant problems, some of which have taken months, even years, to overcome. Furthermore, governing bodies have now a far greater responsibility for decision-making in such situations. In many parts of the country good applicants for headteacher posts are becoming increasingly difficult to find; and why should we, some governors may think, lose our good headteacher to an LEA secondment and have to face the daunting prospect of finding and working with a temporary substitute?

There is a strong possibility, then, that LEAs who wish to follow the path of finding full-time appraisers for headteachers will make appoint-ments rather than seek agreement from governing bodies for secondments, looking particularly towards those who are within a few years of retirement.

One issue here is that many secondary headteachers so appointed would, if they were not to be financially disadvantaged, have to be placed on salary scales that made them senior to, for example, all advisers other than the chief adviser, a situation that would not be without repercussions for the good relations of CEOs with their professional staff. Another issue is that the advent into the LEA structure of a number of such postholders directly from long experience of management 'from their side of the fence' may well lead to problems of assimilation with existing LEA staff.

The alternative proposal is also not without its problems. At a time when open enrolment under the conditions of the Education Reform Act 1988 is forcing schools into the competitive mode, into 'marketing' as the profession is reluctantly learning to call it, the selection of peer appraisers is a matter of considerable delicacy. In circumstances other than those imposed on headteachers by the present climate, there would be much to be said for peer appraisers being selected from within primary and secondary consortia of schools. There would be an expectation of greater understanding of the issues of the immediate neighbourhood; local colleagues would be better known and their presence in the school would be less of a threat; corporate approaches to issues raised by appraisal would be likely to develop; the role of the appraiser as 'critical friend' would be easier to establish. Yet we have to face realities and accept that for many LEAs in today's climate this is a pipe dream.

The number of peer group headteacher appraisers that will be required, one third of the total number of headteachers in the LEA, poses a further problem. Clearly, newly appointed headteachers are unlikely to be selected: from their point of view selection would be undesirable since they would regard themselves, even if they were already experienced headteachers, as having much to learn in their new LEA or new school or about their new colleagues; and from the LEA's point of view since they would lack credibility with their peers. If those on the verge of retirement and those whose own performance as headteachers render them unlikely choices are removed from consideration, it seems very probable that the LEA will find their field of choice restricted to at best one in two of those eligible. Among these will be a number who will be too heavily committed with other LEA responsibilities to take on this additional role, and others who will prefer not to engage, in the current climate of rapid change and stress, in any commitments beyond those for which they are statutorily responsible.

It is therefore not too far-fetched to suggest that there will be some LEAs with too few headteachers willing and able to take on this role to make peer appraisal viable; and these LEAs will perforce have to opt for the superintendent model. Alternatively, LEAs and the DES may find unworkable the recommendation of para 23 that a serving headteacher 'should not be involved in the appraisal programme of more than three other headteachers at any one time'. Indeed, it has already been observed that, on a biennial appraisal cycle, the time cost for the peer appraiser is not evenly balanced between the two years and that an increase to four appraisals which 'Box and Cox' would not be unduly burdensome.

We would not wish to make too much of these difficulties, though it would be poor management of the innovation if they were not given full consideration before decisions were taken which all parties might regret. If the introduction of appraisal is phased in over a number of years, as we are led to believe will be the case, there will come on line a succession of headteachers who, having themselves been through a biennial cycle and having gained experience of appraising within their own schools, will have the confidence and experience to take on the appraiser role for their own peer colleagues. At the same time it must be recognised that experience as appraiser within one's own school and as peer appraisee contributes to but does not equate with understanding of the role of peer appraiser. There would be a grave danger of the dilution of the necessary skills if this kind of cascade model were of itself considered all that was required.

The total time commitment for peer appraisers for their role in each headteacher appraisal is, we calculate, four to five days, possibly diminishing to three to four in the second and subsequent cycles. Details of how that estimate is arrived at are included in the sections which follow.

COMPONENTS OF HEADTEACHER APPRAISAL

Whether the appraisers are superintendent or peer, they will need to familiarise themselves with the circumstances of each school. This is not to be confused with data collection, much of which will be the responsibility of the CEO's officer or adviser. Rather it is because it is necessary for the appraiser to view the school in the light of its own management style, structure and circumstances and not to apply to it extraneous criteria.

Some idea of the context and the manner in which the school operates will be gleaned from a reading of the school's development plan, which will include a statement of its aims and objectives; of the staff handbook; of information prepared for parents at various stages of a pupil's passage through the school; and possibly of newsletters and other similar public materials. We would expect this activity, certainly for a secondary school, to occupy the appraiser for at least half a day. Ideally it should be followed by a discussion with the appraisee in which there can be further elucidation. However, it is more likely that, with time a valuable commodity, such a discussion will be incorporated in the initial meeting, for which a further half day must be allocated.

Initial Meeting

If there is not to be suspicion on the part of the appraisee that, in some covert way, judgments are being made, it is essential that there is open behaviour and agreement over the way information will be collected:

> The clarification of sources and methods of collecting information for the appraisal [is] a particularly important function of this meeting for heads, given the diversity of their work.
>
> (DES, 1989a, para 51)

Furthermore, because it is clear that an appraisal interview can be no more than a sampling procedure, it is important that particular areas of focus are established and agreed. There are two arguments against the selection of these areas of focus at the beginning of the biennial cycle that we would like to refute.

The first is that, if headteachers know what they are being appraised on, they will bend all their energies to these targets at the expense of others. This is both cynical and unrealistic. Headteachers are nowadays required to manage highly complex institutions and cannot afford to let their management priorities become subordinated to mere self-interest. Furthermore, all managerial tasks are interdependent and the weakening of effort in one direction would undoubtedly have repercussions in others.

The second, a more reasonable argument, is that priorities may change over the biennnial cycle. Although the selection should in fact be made not on priorities but on aspects of the headteacher's role which will give a broad view of managerial competency, there is no reason why there should not be a modification of the appraisal goals if this is the wish and in the best interest of the appraisee.

The selection of more than three areas of focus is counterproductive. In an appraisal interview of a headteacher it is extremely unlikely that the discussion of any major topic will take less than half an hour. No item of the appraisal agenda should be dealt with cursorily because time presses. If the true purposes of appraisal are to be met then it should be borne in mind that:

> There is . . . benefit to be gained from the examination in depth of a few specific areas, provided that the selection is balanced and that key aspects of the head's work are not neglected over a long period.
>
> (para 52)

Self-appraisal

This activity is as important for headteachers as for all other members of staff. In one sense it is more important, since managerial goals are often long term and achievement may be less easy to evaluate. Headteachers, occupied as they are with the introduction of major innovations alongside dealing with day-to-day crises, can easily lose sight of their successes.

Although its use is recommended by the NSG (para 53) we have serious doubts about the applicability to headteachers of the proforma set out in Appendix B of the ACAS report. It is possible that some headteachers will not need any kind of proforma or prompt list, but for those who do we have devised one which is shown in Figure 10.1. It is not intended to be worked through from beginning to end, but rather to act as a series of reminders of areas of focus on which the headteacher might like to comment in preparation for the appraisal interview. Indeed, there is some merit in its more frequent, personal use, since it acts as a reminder of things achieved and may therefore be very reassuring. Those who have trialled it confirm that it acts as a useful focus for their consideration of their own performance.

Collection of information

The NSG report cites (para 54) the following sources of information useful to appraisers:

- publicly available data relating to the work of the school;
- task and/or classroom observation;
- interviews with staff, governors and parents;
- consultation with LEA officers and advisers.

Publicly available data

Some of this will have been covered in the peer appraiser's preparatory work. Other information will be known to the liaison adviser, described variously as the 'patch' adviser, pastoral adviser, consortium adviser or such other title as the LEA has coined. How public is *public*? We would suggest that *professionally available* is a better term, since the data must of necessity include matters about staffing, for example, not known to the public, or matters the knowledge of which is restricted to governors. Many authorities have recently become aware, as a consequence of the Education Reform Act and, in particular, the introduction of appraisal, that there are serious shortcomings in the communications system between the liaison adviser and phase and subject specialist advisers and advisory teachers. Some LEAs have begun to use information technology to remedy this defect.

Figure 10.1 Prompt list: headteacher self-appraisal

For each of the headings below where *in the period under review* you believe you have had a significant role, list the goal(s) which you set yourself. Assess the extent to which you have *so far* succeeded in meeting those goals.

What circumstances have helped you?
What have hindered you?

THE DEVELOPMENT OF . . .

- the school as a centre of learning
- the school as a caring institution
- the quality and contribution of the staff through in-service training and other means
- the managerial structure and style of the school

RELATIONSHIPS WITH . . .

- staff, both teaching and ancillary
- parents
- the governing body
- the LEA
- the neighbourhood or community

THE MANAGEMENT OF . . .

- the school budget
- the school fabric

LIAISON WITH . . .

- other schools and educational institutions to which pupils go/from which pupils come
- local business and industry

AND FINALLY . . .

- your personal development in this post
- any other goals

Of these, which do you regard as the area which has given you the most satisfaction? Which the least satisfaction?

© Routledge 1991

Task and/or classroom observation

Except for those primary headteachers of small schools who have a full or nearly full timetable commitment, we can see little merit in classroom observation, unless the headteacher should specifically request it. The only plausible ground for such a request, we believe, is where the headteacher wishes to demonstrate to staff credibility as a practitioner; and in such cases we suggest that the observer might well be the curriculum coordinator or head of department of the subject being taught.

Task observation is another matter. For this, *shadowing* is one possibility. This entails the peer appraiser or the adviser accompanying the headteacher for a full day, or, better still, several half days, recording – with agreement – activities and their outcomes and at the end of the period sharing impressions. This is a strategy used by many researchers (Richardson, 1973; Lyons, 1974; Hall *et al.*, 1986) which participants have found valuable as a learning experience and often very revealing of the way they manage time.

Another strategy is for the headteacher to nominate a particular activity to be observed over a number of occasions. This might well be the introduction of a new practice in management: the first stage being the presentation to staff, giving the appraiser an opportunity to observe the way in which the headteacher conducts a meeting; continuing by means of a log maintained by the headteacher and made available to the appraiser of relevant discussions and decisions since the initial presentation; and concluding with the meeting at which decisions are reached or promulgated. This is, of course, a time-consuming activity; but given that the local adviser would expect to visit the school on a number of occasions in any case, this might not so much add to that number as give further purpose to the visits.

Interviews with staff, governors and parents

We have serious reservations as to the propriety or efficacy of this strategy for the collection of information. First, we are dubious that it will contribute significantly to the data being collected, since there will not be the time for interviews with a representative sample of any of these groups, in particular of parents. Secondly, while the Code of Practice (see Appendix 1) is excellent as guidance for interviewers, and its purpose well understood by professionals, it will be very difficult to impose upon lay interviewees. Thirdly, we do not think it accords with the principle of open behaviour which we have advocated as essential to any appraisal system if these interviews do not take place in the presence of the headteacher; but, for parents in particular and for some staff, that may in itself be inhibiting.

We do not doubt that it is important that the voices of these groups are heard. Indeed, we are surprised at the exclusion of the prime client group of the school, the pupils. We suggest, however, that there are other, more general ways of collecting information from these groups: through an open staff meeting about general issues facing the staff; through the governors' meetings which liaison advisers or other representatives of the CEO will attend as a normal part of their duties; through the annual meeting for the school parent body or, more advantageously since they will undoubtedly be better attended and more representative, open or report evenings; and through a visit to classes to glean the impressions of pupils. In all these situations control of the observation of the Code of Practice rests with the appraisers. Except for the governors' meeting, at which the presence of peer appraisers would be *ultra vires*, the attendance of either appraiser will be readily accepted or will pass unnoticed.

Consultation with LEA officers and advisers

We have already indicated on page 168 that LEAs need to devise, if they are not already in existence, effective systems for the collation of the written – and, we trust, open – comments by members of the CEO's advisory staff on visits to the school. Some of these visits will be formal, as when performance indicators are being used to evaluate a school's performance. Others will be less formal, as advisers and advisory teachers act in a supportive way to aid the school in its development: its introduction of new key stages of the National Curriculum, for example, or of Local Financial Management. There will, however, on occasions be the need to ask a particular officer or adviser for a specific update of information, especially where the key result area being appraised lies within a specialist field. The way in which Special Educational Needs are being coped with in the school is one instance; its Personal, Social and Health Education programme another. It is important that the local adviser acts as a filter so that the peer appraiser is not overloaded with irrelevant information. Equally, he or she must be well informed on those areas which are on the agenda for the appraisal interview.

Length of data collection period

It is difficult to follow the reasoning of the NSG in the recommendation (para 59) that the length of the data collection period 'should not normally be longer than one term'. Understandably, the data should not include matters about which all concerned will have to delve into their memories, but many managerial activities of necessity spread over quite lengthy periods. If one of the purposes of appraisal is to enable the appraisee to assess the appropriateness of a sequence of activities, there is little point in restricting the data to the most recent events. The management of innovation follows a well established cycle: Planning – Preparation – Performance – Evaluation – Stabilisation. It is unrealistic to appraise the headteacher's role in that process by looking only at that part which took place in a restricted period of time.

Conclusion

It is accepted that most of the data collection will be the responsibility of the local adviser. Nevertheless, the peer appraiser must have some direct observation to bring to the appraisal interview, occupying in aggregate at least a day, and must also spend some time with the adviser, both to discuss the data and to plan the agenda and strategy for the appraisal interview itself. Finally, it is advisable for both appraisers to be present when the agenda is agreed with the appraisee, even though this may prove to be a mere formality.

The appraisal interview

This is rightly regarded as 'the central feature of appraisal for headteachers, as it has been for teachers' (para 57). It should be conducted by the peer appraiser. The local adviser is thus free to take notes from which the appraisal statement will be prepared and is likely to intervene only in order to give information, clarify a situation or correct a misapprehension. Over many years of experience in interviewing we have come to appreciate that, in a duologue, after a short time the presence of a third party goes unnoticed, particularly when that person is already well-known to the other two. On the other hand, being questioned by two or more very rapidly takes the 'conversation with a purpose' into the realms of an inquisition, in which interviewees rapidly find themselves adjusting their responses to the questioner rather than the questions. The formal interview that is part of most staffing appointments, for example, is likened by many at the receiving end to a game or competition in which their task is to satisfy the expectations of the interviewers, sometimes even the differing expectations of different interviewers, rather than to set their educational philosophy and skills in the balance against the demands of the post. The climate and the purpose of the appraisal interview must therefore be firmly established in the minds of all the participants. It must be remembered too that headteachers have, as appraisers, established their personal styles for the appraisals they have conducted and will therefore have certain expectations of how their own appraisals will be conducted. It is therefore important that the process is clearly explained and understood.

We reiterate, even more strongly if that is possible, our view that 'professional targets for action' (para 49) should be agreed, not at the appraisal interview, but on a separate occasion. That there will be some

identification at the appraisal interview of actions to be taken and goals set
– by no means the same thing – we accept. However, we remain
convinced, as do most of those with whom we have worked, that it is
asking too much of appraisees to focus in the same interview both on the
appraisal of the activities of the previous biennium and on the identification
of goals for that to come.

The appraisal statement

It follows from what we have suggested as the key role for advisers in the
appraisal interview that they are the ones best placed to draw up the
appraisal statement. This should be done without delay while the interview
is fresh in the minds of all three participants. The draft needs to be
considered by the peer appraiser and then agreed by the appraisee in the
presence of both. It is now that it becomes possible to begin to consider
goalsetting, since agreement on the statement may be no more than a
formality; but we would still sound a note of caution, since the climate
may well continue to be retrospective rather than prospective and possibly
not yet right for establishing future targets.

Follow-up and formal review meeting

As with other members of staff, this is an important element of the
appraisal process. Follow-up, however, is less easy to bring about
informally, certainly for the peer appraiser. Ideally one would like to see
the concept of the 'critical friend' take root, whereby appraisees develop a
relationship with their peer appraisers that enables them to contact them on
the phone and ask for a meeting to tease out some particular issue that is
associated with their previous appraisal or their current goals. For many
headteachers the role is a lonely one and it is undoubtedly of benefit to
share difficulties and successes; but the long history of the concept of
'captain of the ship', solely responsible for all that happens therein, even to
the extent of going down with it rather than sending out a Mayday signal,
dies hard. The more exacting the demands of the teaching profession, the
more we ought to be looking at ways of breaking down traditional
isolationism.

The formal review is easier to establish as a procedure. Without in any
way attempting to conduct a mini-appraisal, the appraisers need to explore
with the appraisee the way in which progress to declared goals is going.
The appraisee should regard this as an opportunity: to point out
unanticipated constraints, to seek resources, to discuss further training
needs that have arisen since the appraisal and to test out perceptions of the
progress that is being made.

We have seen in the past decade many of the barriers between
headteacher colleagues breaking down, so that the sharing of problems is

becoming more commonplace. Regrettably we still see too many examples of the lack of mutual understanding and respect between headteachers and advisers, often caused by a lack of appreciation on the part of the former of the tremendous increase in the range of tasks required of advisers and, despite the excellent work of the Centre for Adviser and Inspector Development (CAID) at Woolley Hall, of inadequate in-service training for advisers. Headteacher appraisal conducted by advisers and headteachers may do much to improve this relationship, as the two arms of the education service are seen increasingly as interdependent.

THE SCHOOL DEVELOPMENT PLAN

While it is important to distinguish between the appraisal of the headteacher and the review or audit of the school development plan (DES, 1990a), there is nevertheless a symbiotic relationship between the two. The school development plan is the joint responsibility of the staff and in particular the headteacher, the governing body and the LEA. It has to conform to the conditions set by both local and central government, but at the same time must reflect the distinctive nature of the neighbourhood in which the school physically exists and the community with which it relates and which it must serve. It is incumbent on every school to have a development plan and on every governing body and LEA to review it periodically. The ability of the institution to deliver the development plan is conditioned by the material and human resources available to it.

It is within this context that the appraisal of all staff necessarily falls. Their successes as teachers and managers will lead to the successful implementation of the development plan. For the classroom teacher some immediate goals will be easily perceived as relating to specific areas of the development plan: curriculum development leading to the introduction and consolidation of the National Curriculum is an obvious example. There will, however, be other areas of the development plan which they will perceive as relevant to the school as an institution but not so readily identifiable in terms of personal goals: the implementation of local management of schools, for example.

Those with senior managerial responsibility, and particularly the headteacher, have a heightened perception of these long-term goals, since they relate more particularly to the areas of management for which they are responsible. Yet no individual, not even the headteacher, can be appraised on institutional goals. They are appraised on their agreed and contracted contribution to the realisation of that whole school policy, not on the success or failure of the implementation of that policy.

One important reason for making this plain is that no LEA is likely to have the manpower to conduct development plan reviews to coincide with the biennial appraisal cycle; indeed, even if there were the human resources, we would question whether the enterprise was worth undertaking, since taking the watch to pieces to see what makes it tick usually results in its failure as an accurate timepiece. What is needed, however, is a temporal relationship between the appraisal of the headteacher and the review of the school development plan.

One LEA is currently proposing a cycle on these lines:

Year 1: School Development Review
Year 2: Headteacher Appraisal
Year 3: Review Update
Year 4: Headteacher Appraisal

The review update would be undertaken by the local or phase adviser and would utilise the feedback from curriculum area and other visitations over the previous biennium. This interweaving of the personal element, the appraisal of the headteacher, with the institutional element, the review of the school development plan, brings into correct focus the relationship between the two, while making clear that they have different objectives.

Chapter 11

Other issues

SUPPORT TEACHERS

The NSG report recommends that LEAs 'should be required to make arrangements for the appraisal of all those on teachers' conditions of service'. This is only commonsense, since most advisory teachers are on short-term appointments and expect to return to the classroom at a later stage in their careers. Furthermore, it would be an anomaly if certain specialist and peripatetic teachers not based in schools but nevertheless working extensively in schools were excluded from the appraisal process.

The work of support teachers has diversified considerably in recent years, largely through curriculum innovations inspired or supported by central government: TVEI, IT, CDT, for example. In many LEAs the number of support teachers has greatly increased, in spite of the fact that some have had to cut back on peripatetic music or special needs teachers. The main thrust of the NSG recommendation (para 48) is this:

> The [support] teacher should wherever possible be appraised by a person who already has management responsibility for him or her; and the appraisal programme should include task observation related to the teacher's job [specification], together with pre- and post-observation.

Line management appraisal

In most LEAs and for most support teachers the line manager will be a specialist adviser. Two issues are likely to arise, however. In some subject areas or large LEAs the team of support teachers in a particular discipline may well be beyond the four recommended as the maximum for one appraiser to appraise, but nevertheless be in line management to one adviser. It would be excessively doctrinaire if the recommendation had to be rigidly adhered to: this is not a situation that can be compared with, for example, a large department in a school where appraisals could be shared with a second in command. At the other end of the spectrum are those support teachers who plough a lone furrow, directly responsible not to a line manager with responsibility for their specialism, but to the chief adviser or to a senior adviser to whom has been delegated responsibility for the whole range of support work.

Task observation

The temptation to draw a parallel between *task observation* of support teachers and *classroom observation* of full-time school staff must be resisted. The role of many support teachers is primarily to service those teachers whose knowledge of content or methodology in a given subject area falls short of what is needed, either because the area is innovatory or because headteachers or local advisers have detected weaknesses. Support may be through in-service education in any of its many forms; or it may be through observation, shadowing, co-teaching or even by demonstration lessons. The task, therefore, needs to be viewed as a complexity, with strands relating to the specific needs of the curriculum, the school and the individual teacher; and the managerial aspects of what is being observed are crucial features of the appraisal.

The task observation consequently needs to address itself to performance criteria that relate to but are by no means identical with those appropriate to the class teacher. Indeed, it is highly problematic whether a set of generic performance criteria can be established for support teachers, so varied are their roles and consequent job specifications. Sandwell LEA, very much in the vanguard in considering the practicalities of appraising support teachers, has gone to great pains to draw up what they prefer to call a *prompt sheet* of quantifiable and qualitative indicators. The LEA wisely sounds two notes of warning: the first, that quantifiable indicators 'could lead to very crude, insensitive appraisals of performance'; the second, that all such lists have their limitations because there is the temptation to seek conformity when the great strength of support teachers is their ability to respond to situations as they find them.

Briefing for task observation

This must be fundamentally different from that for a classroom observation. It is highly probable that the line manager will already have been involved in the identification of the task and will have shared with the support team or teacher the strategies whereby the task may be accomplished. The aims and expectations, and the means of realising them, will therefore not be comparable with those contained in a lesson preparation, but will relate to the task as a whole.

An illustration may clarify the issue. In one of the LEA's primary schools the headteacher has expressed concern to the local adviser over the ability of her staff to cope with the requirements of the National Curriculum in science teaching. She has a willing staff but nobody has any higher qualification in science than an O level obtained in the distant past. The science adviser agrees that the situation is grave enough to warrant the presence in that school of a member of the science support team for a day a week for, initially, half a term. A range of strategies is discussed: help with materials and lesson preparation; some direct instruction in the curriculum content; some co-teaching; and, when the teachers have gained confidence, some lesson observation and criticism. What is eventually agreed as potentially the most effective and acceptable intervention becomes the overall task of the support teacher.

It is inconceivable that, for the support teacher's appraisal, this task as a whole could be observed. At best, by observing one of the activities that are the components of the task, the appraiser may get a snapshot of the degree to which the appraisee has been successful in achieving the agreed aims of the intervention. The support teacher might therefore be observed anywhere along a spectrum from running an in-service session for the teachers in this school to sitting in on a class and himself debriefing the teacher on the conduct of the lesson.

On the one hand, then, the management process needs to be observed, whereby the support teacher creates the climate in which initially his support is welcomed and valued and whereby eventually he is able to withdraw, leaving the class teacher confident in his ownership of new skills and knowledge. This, it is highly probable, will be best observed by the local adviser of the school. On the other hand, the skills and knowledge of the support teacher need to be appraised; and for this the expertise of the subject adviser is required.

From this scenario we would draw two conclusions: that it will often be appropriate for two advisers to be involved in the task observation of a support teacher; the other that this observation, together with adequate briefing and debriefing, could not be accomplished in less than the equivalent of a full working day, considerably more than that required for classroom observation.

Data collection

It is advisable that, as for class teachers, the data is recent and that the task observation has taken place as near to the appraisal interview as possible. However, because support teachers generally move rapidly from school to school and task to task, the collection of data is far less straightforward than for a class teacher. Some data can be derived from the support teachers' logs: the number of schools visited, of staff supported, of courses and workshops run. The evaluation of courses and workshops should, as for all trainers, be a routine procedure, but with the *caveat* that measures of the effects of training on those trained are more easily come by than measures of effectiveness on the trainees' future performance.

There are a number of possible sources for subjective evaluation of the effectiveness of support teachers as change agents: the views of the classroom teachers themselves, their line managers, headteachers and other senior staff, and local and specialist advisers. The code of practice (Appendix 1) is as relevant to the appraisal of support staff as to that of the classroom teacher; adherence to it is perhaps even more important, if only because the diversity of their work offers more opportunity for incorrect procedures in the collection of data.

THE ROLE OF ADVISERS AND INSPECTORS

It is interesting that the final sentence of the NSG paragraph (48) on the appraisal of support teachers reads: 'Wherever possible, the appraisers of the [support] teachers should themselves be within an appraisal scheme.' There should be no dissent from this view and some LEAs have already set up schemes for the appraisal of all officers and advisers, arguing rightly that the credibility of their appraisal schemes for the teachers in schools is much enhanced by the perception that central staff have similar experiences. However, neither the NSG report nor this book has within its remit the appraisal of educationists other than teachers. This section concerns itself, therefore, with the role of advisers and inspectors in school appraisal. In it we will argue that, whatever arrangements are made for their own training as appraisers and appraisees, they need extensive training for the areas in which they will be involved that relate to the appraisal of teachers.

What advisers and inspectors actually do has changed considerably in recent years. Winkley (1985), after a very thorough survey of the service, concluded that from the mid-1970s there had been a steady role shift towards a more clearly defined inspectorial function. Since he wrote, that shift has become even more pronounced. This is rarely as a consequence of a deliberate change of policy on the part of LEAs but is a reactive change as more and more surveys and other inspectorial tasks fill their days, bind them to their office desks, deny them the opportunity to visit schools and, in the words of a headteacher in a survey by Hellawell (1990), 'to view the school from the point of view of no particular target specification, merely to *feel* the school'.

Despite the move towards more inspectorial functions, there remains a widespread preference for the title of adviser for two probable reasons: the first that there is already in HMI a body of inspectors centrally administered and quite independent of LEAs and it is undesirable that there should be any confusion between their role and that of the LEA personnel; the second that schools, already resistant to the increased inspectorial functions devolving on the LEA, are likely to be further antagonised by and suspicious of any change of name.

If for no other reason than brevity, we intend to use the term *adviser* throughout this section. The recommended role for advisers permeates the NSG report, sometimes explicitly but more often implicitly. We detect seven areas of involvement.

The appraisal of support teachers

This has been sufficiently covered in the previous section. All that needs to be said is that this is the one area in which advisers will have sole responsibility for appraising fellow professionals. In all other areas they will either be working in partnership with others or be involved in activities that are consequent on teacher appraisal.

Support for schools in meeting in-service and staff development needs that arise as a consequence of the appraisal process

This will at first glance appear to be an area in which advisers are already well equipped to act; yet the significance of the changes of the ways in which support now needs to be delivered, following new funding arrangements for in-service education through LEATGS and the introduction of LFM, will have to be carefully thought through. Advisers find themselves having to adjudicate between two sets of needs: the general needs of the teaching force in their specialism and the specific needs of a school. They may well find themselves having to say to schools that specific needs can be met only from the school's own in-service budget; and, since this is almost certain to be under considerable pressure from other internal demands, they may at times find themselves having to insist that training needs that are an outcome of the appraisal process are given due priority. If this does not happen then the high profile which the pilot LEAs and the National Steering Group sought to give to the staff development component of appraisal will be dissipated.

Mediation between appraiser and appraisee when there is disagreement over the wording of the appraisal report

Adjudication when a teacher insists on the right to be appraised by someone other than the designated line manager

It is here that the need for counselling and negotiating skills becomes most evident. Provided that appraisal is regarded as primarily concerned with the improvement of performance and not with assessment, there will be few occasions when the adviser will be called upon to mediate, since conflicts of this kind are best and most usually resolved within the school itself. However, if any external factor appears to enter the equation – the award of merit pay or a situation in which the number of staff in a school has to be reduced, for example – then we may well see a growing perception, whether justified or not, that there is the need to invoke appeal procedures.

Support for headteachers in their presentation to governors of the outcomes of staff appraisal

LEAs differ widely in their choice of official representative at governors' meetings. There is now no necessity for them to provide even a clerk, but most LEAs take the view that the increased powers and responsibilities of governing bodies make it imperative that the CEO is represented at meetings by someone with the requisite knowledge to advise on procedures and, where necessary, support the school staff. Increasingly LEAs have devised schemes whereby a family of schools is allocated to an adviser. Some LEAs – Dudley is one – allocate a pair of advisers with complementary skills to a larger group of primary and secondary schools within an organisational support structure, called, in that example, a development group. Leicestershire pairs an adviser with an education officer. There is no doubt that the practice, costly of LEA staff time though it may be, is a valuable support for headteachers and their staff. The issue of the rights and powers of governors in relation to appraisal is complex and is dealt with in the next section. All that is needed here is to signal that, when LEAs draw up guidelines for governing bodies to enable them to discharge their public responsibilities for teacher appraisal, they must ensure that there is also training for advisers that enables them to offer governors appropriate professional advice as to what does and what does not lie within their remit.

Participation in the appraisal of headteachers

The role of the adviser in the appraisal of headteachers is crucial but by no means easy to delineate in spite of the recommendations of the NSG report (paras 49–60). There is no doubt that these recommendations have sought to reconcile the requirement of headteachers that their appraisal be conducted by someone with recent and relevant experience of headship and the need to convey to the outside world that headteacher appraisal is not conducted within a closed circle of peers.

Headteachers do not see themselves in line management to advisers. This has long been known to be true of secondary headteachers, but a survey of primary headteacher opinion (Hellawell, 1990) revealed that only three of twenty-four respondents felt themselves to be accountable to LEA advisers. Yet, in what seems to be a contradiction to that view, asked 'who do you think would be *in a position* [our italics] to carry out an appraisal of primary headteachers like yourself?' fifteen respondents named LEA advisers, only one fewer than named fellow heads.

There has been in the past a view frequently expressed by headteachers that as professionals they were accountable to themselves. When pressed on this point they were likely to take refuge in generalities, citing the LEA, which as an organisation cannot be regarded as a manager but as a management agency, or the CEO, who is only their manager in a symbolic sense.

We do not believe that this view is now widely held. All teachers, headteachers not least, are beginning to recognise that recent legislation has created the means whereby their very professionality is in danger of being undermined. There is therefore a need to see the profession as a unity, of teachers and administrators in tandem. The NSG recommendation for headteacher appraisal, that it should be conducted jointly by a peer headteacher and an adviser, with the latter having a significant role in data collection, is not merely a safeguard that appraisal remains a professional responsibility; it is also a means by which the relationship between school and LEA can be further cemented.

The proposed partnership both removes the concern that headteachers have felt over the possibility of being appraised by those without personal experience of headship and emphasises the duality of responsibility that headteachers have: to the school and, recent legislation not withstanding, to the LEA. A clear distinction between the roles of the two appraisers may not be as easy to maintain as the NSG report appears to imply; but if advisers can in general hold firm to the task of obtaining, collating and sharing with the headteacher appraiser the data relevant to the appraisal and leave the conduct of the appraisal interview largely in the hands of the peer appraiser, then the collaboration should work effectively.

It would be unwise, however, to assume that this will happen without training. As discussed earlier (Chapter 10, p. 168), the NSG report (para 54) cites four sources for data collection:

- publicly available data relating to the work of the school;
- task and/or classroom observation;
- interviews with staff, governors and parents;
- consultation with LEA officers and advisers.

Of these it is the third that is most likely to lead to misunderstanding and even conflict. The NSG report draws attention to the Code of Practice (reproduced in Appendix 1) and states that the collection of information must 'be handled with sensitivity'. We suggest that one element of the training in appraisal for advisers ought to include the study of some hypothetical statements obtained in this category, not merely to see whether or not they accord formally with the Code of Practice, but more importantly to investigate what might be the repercussions of their presentation to the peer appraiser and eventually the appraisee.

DATA COLLECTION

The collection of data for headteacher appraisal demands of the LEA adviser and peer appraiser delicate judgments. How do you respond to the following scenarios in the light of the Code of Practice, both letter and spirit?

Peer appraiser to adviser

I would welcome your advice. A colleague at work is a parent governor at Linden Road. She knows that the head's appraisal is due soon and has asked to see me – I wonder how she knows I am the peer appraiser? – on behalf of the parents about 'an important matter which they feel must be on the agenda'. She hasn't as yet been more precise, but I am sure this has to do with his multi-faith assemblies. I cannot refuse to see her, but is this relevant to our appraisal? Her information will be well documented. She is that kind of person!

Headteacher to appraiser

Yes, I *have* seen the list of background information I'm supposed to supply for my appraisal*, but I'm sorry, I simply haven't the time for all that paperwork.
(* see Para 16 of the Code of Practice)

Teacher governor to visiting peer appraiser

Much as I like and respect the head I have to say this. Staff meetings are a farce. She gives talks at the Teachers' Centre for the LEA on collegiate management but in our school she and the deputy have always got it all cut and dried in advance. We're just a rubber stamp. I've mentioned our feelings to her a number of times, but all she does is offer to discuss the agenda with me before the meetings. Bully for me, but that won't cut any ice with the staff! Can you get this on the agenda for the appraisal interview? It might help to clear the air.

Memo from Chair of Governors to LEA adviser

Governors have a major role to play in headteacher appraisal. I am concerned that there be general consensus rather than run the risk of individual approaches from governors to the appraisal team. Accordingly I am asking the Clerk to include discussion of [the headteacher]'s performance on the agenda of the next meeting. Teacher governors will of course have to withdraw while this item is discussed. The head has a right to be present, I take it. Nevertheless his presence may inhibit discussion and I suggest that he too should withdraw.

© Routledge 1991

Follow-up, both formal and informal, is no less important for headteacher appraisal than for teacher appraisal. The involvement of the peer appraiser in formal follow-up should be a routine matter of allocating time and deciding a suitable occasion for preliminary discussion between the appraisers, the follow-up interview itself and a debriefing session. Informal follow-up will present greater problems. For peer appraisers, unless they are in full-time secondment, there is the problem of making time to meet the needs of the appraisee. The concept of peer appraiser in the role of 'critical friend' (Wallace, 1986) is good in principle but depends on availability. The adviser, though probably no less overworked, is probably better placed to organise his time for the informal follow-up during normal school visits.

Development plan review

Although the name by which this is known will differ from LEA to LEA, there is a common responsibility for conducting a periodic review or audit of each school's development plan (DES, 1990). In most LEAs, advisers, singly or in teams, will have a programme of formal school visits for the purpose of establishing and reporting on the extent to which a school has been able to achieve what it has set out to do. Performance indicators may have a place in this process, though it has to be said that there is some cynicism in the profession about their value, since they appear to ignore the unique conditions under which any educational institution works. In our view, of far greater importance is the long-term relationship that needs to be built up between the school and the advisory team.

We have indicated earlier (Figure 7.1, page 110) the importance of the balance between whole school policy and personal and professional development. It would be wrong, however, to view policy as if it were inscribed on stone tablets. While the principles underlying the policy may well remain unchanged, both the means of implementing it and the priorities within it will be subject to review in the light of internal and external pressures. However expert as managers of change headteachers and senior staff may be, there is a need for the detached view, either to ratify or to moderate that from within the institution.

For the appraisal of the headteacher, certainly, and for that of other staff with significant managerial responsibility in schools which have or are developing corporate management styles, the development plan review provides important data. It is sensible, therefore, if it is timed so that it can make the maximum contribution. First, its periodicity should, if possible, conform with that of the appraisal cycle. Few LEAs will be able to afford a biennial review of all primary and secondary schools, but a full review every four years should be within the capacity of the advisory team, with a biennial mini-review and follow-up.

It is difficult to forecast how precisely the review will mesh with the school's appraisal cycle. Some schools, particularly small schools, will, we forecast, decide to appraise all the staff in alternate years; but that intention may easily be modified by staff changes so that over a period of time this becomes the pattern but with variations. Large schools may feel that the impact of appraising all staff in the one year is excessive and prefer a roll-over programme which will enable them to control that impact. There will not be tidy solutions that will enable the LEA review always to take place at the optimum time for the benefit of the school. What is important is that there should be negotiation with the school to establish at what stage in the appraisal process the review would be most helpful.

Certainly the review or the follow-up should have taken place before the headteacher's appraisal. It will have then provided valuable data which can be shared with the peer appraiser and contribute to the drawing up of an effective agenda.

GOVERNORS

There can surely be no aspect of appraisal where there has been more confusion and concern than that concerning the role of governors. The NSG is quite clear as to its stance. In a key section of its report (para 8) it states unequivocally:

> We recognise the important new management responsibilities which the governing bodies of individual schools are shortly to acquire, following the Education Reform Act 1988 . . . It is nevertheless our firm view that statutory responsibility under the Regulations for securing the appraisal of teachers in schools maintained by LEAs should reside with those authorities.

This statement has been welcomed almost universally.

It did not accord, however, with the policy of the executive of the National Association of Managers and Governors (NAGM) which had submitted a position statement in June 1989 to the NSG and was 'unequivocal in its view that school governors should contribute to teacher appraisal' (TES, 1989a). In its submission NAGM had stated that:

> comments and evidence from governors should be tabled in notes via the chair and another governor, and signed by the governor making the comment . . . Comments should have been made earlier by the governor concerned in person to the head.

Their spokesperson observed: 'governors have got to be in there somewhere' (TES, 1989a).

We believe that this statement did considerable harm to the developing understanding of the new relationship between schools, LEAs and governing bodies. Exactly where the balance of accountability lies under the Education Reform Act remains problematic and is constantly being tested as issues arise. Ultimately, whether through the courts, by negotiation or as determined by 'custom and practice', workable case law will be established. Leonard (1988) succinctly identifies the basic issue:

> The Act gives power to governors while leaving (in non-aided schools) the legal responsibilities firmly with the Authority . . . Thus the governors have the rights of an employer, while the LEA has the responsibilities of an employer.

Were governors able to contribute to the appraisal of individual teachers in the haphazard way put forward by the NAGM, they would be doing considerable harm to the whole appraisal process. In schools with which we have been involved we have always valued the contribution of governors, and their approbation of or concerns about what the *school* as an institution has been doing have always been well received; but teacher appraisal is a professional matter, and we are convinced that governors would be going beyond their rights and into the realms of the LEA's responsibilities if they sought to make unstructured, personal and undoubtedly subjective interventions in the appraisal process.

The governing body, as distinct from individual governors, does however have a significant and valuable role in the appraisal process:

> Proposals for action deriving from appraisal should be reported to the governing body of the school if they require an executive decision by that body, or if they relate to resources for which the governing body has specific responsibility.

> (NSG report, para 66)

We conjecture that there has been much discussion, and doubtless some intensive lobbying since the publication of the NSG report, about the role of governors in appraisal. Certainly the draft National Framework, and particularly the accompanying supplementary guidance, are far more explicit and detailed than the NSG report.

Governor participation in the appraisal process

Nothing in the draft National Framework or the supplementary guidance suggests that, for the appraisal of the assistant teacher, governors will be invited to contribute data, unless the appraisee so desires. The components of appraisal for teachers includes 'collection of data from other sources' – other, that is, than classroom observation and, for non-teaching responsibilities, other teachers – *'agreed with the appraisee'* (NF para 11, our italics). For headteachers, however, appraisers are entitled to obtain information from, *inter alia*, 'interviews with staff, governors and parents'

(NF para 25). It should be noted that responsibility for deciding whether and where to seek this information rests with the appraisers, although as will be seen later there is an expectation that the chairperson of governors will be consulted. Clearly neither for assistant teachers nor for the headteacher are governors, individually or collectively, able to insist on contributing to the data. The NAGM argument has evidently been totally rejected.

Governor participation in the appraisal outcomes

This is quite another matter. For assistant teachers 'the headteacher of the school *may* make a copy of the [appraisal] statement available to the chairman of the governors' (para 18, our italics). We believe that it would be wise for a headteacher to make this policy decision in consultation with the staff unless, of course, there were already a binding policy formulated by the teacher unions. Above all, however this decision may be arrived at, it would seem eminently sensible that the appraisal statements of all assistant teachers in the school be treated in identical fashion.

We do not think that a decision to inform the chairperson of governors is a cause for alarm, provided it is clearly understood that the document is confidential. The chairperson is not entitled to convey any part of the statement, verbally or in writing, to any other governor or outside party. If confidentiality is respected, we cannot see that exception can reasonably be taken to this clause. The headteacher and chairperson must be assumed to be working together in the best interest of the school and for this to happen effectively there must be trust and a free flow of relevant information between them. The appraisal statement has been agreed between appraisee and appraiser. If the principle that appraisal is positive and concerned with staff development is observed, then there will be nothing there which could be construed as professionally damaging to the appraisee.

For the headteacher's appraisal statement there is, however, no choice: a copy '*shall* be made available to the chairman of governors of the school' (NF para 29, our italics). It is arguable that this is because headteacher appraisal and school development review are inseparable. In that case it is difficult to see how the availability of the headteacher's appraisal statement can reasonably be restricted to the chairperson. The answer is surely that the statement is in itself irrelevant to the accountability of the headteacher to governors. Their responsibility lies in how they can support him or her in the achievement of the school's policy and short- and long-term goals.

The role of the governing body

This is detailed not in the draft National Framework but in the supplementary guidance which, it must be repeated, is not binding on

LEAs. All the paragraphs merit serious consideration. It is possible for the LEA to 'leave schools discretion over some aspects of detailed arrangements. In such cases it would be appropriate for the governing body to approve the school's arrangements' (SG para 3). We believe that this discretion will rarely be offered or desired, unless absolutely vital to a school's particular circumstances, since teachers, both through their professional associations and through their negotiations with their LEA, will seek through a common framework protection from any possible abuse. Where there is any divergent practice, however, it is proper that the governing body should have the right and responsibility of approving the arrangement.

The governing body has a responsibility 'to make sure that [appraisal] is operating properly in accordance with school and LEA policy and that it is properly integrated into the management of the school' (SG para 47). The governing body should also 'be informed when information is being collected for headteacher appraisal' (SG para 48), a not unreasonable suggestion.

The same paragraph states that 'the chairman of the governing body should have the opportunity to submit comments to the appraiser designed to inform the appraisal interview'. Here there may be some ambiguity. Are the comments solely those of the chairperson or may comments from other governors be sought and collated by the chairperson? The latter would be most unwise. There are grave dangers in the giving of any information that is not within the direct knowledge of the contributor. It is likely that, if unsubstantiated data were offered to the appraisers, they would, as professionals, both ignore it and on future occasions exercise their undoubted right not to seek a contribution from the chairperson.

Far less contentious is the statement that 'when considering schoolwide plans for inservice training and development of staff, governing bodies should have available to them a report by the headteacher on the main messages emerging from appraisal in respect of training and development needs' (SG para 51). One of the great merits of appraisal is that it will provide evidence for the most effective use of INSET funding and will make governors aware of the great need, now and in the foreseeable future, for regular expenditure to enable teachers to maintain and improve their professional standards.

Teacher appraisal and pay

The third report of the Interim Advisory Committee on School Teachers' Pay and Conditions (IAC, 1990) introduced significant new elements of flexibility *at the local level*. Extended local scales may be introduced at the discretion of the LEA or the governors of grant-maintained schools, but not the governors of LMS schools. Incremental enhancements, on the other hand, which give the possibility for increases of up to four multiples of

£250 at incremental points other than the maximum, are at the discretion of LEAs or governing bodies. Not surprisingly, teachers are asking themselves how governing bodies will decide which, if any, members of staff should be entitled to these enhancements. The government, we have been assured repeatedly, has ruled out any direct link between merit pay and teacher appraisal. Nevertheless, one feels to be in humpty-dumpty land when a government minister, Alan Howarth, is quoted as stating at a NUT conference (TES, 1990a):

> Decisions about individual teachers' careers, and their pay, are very important . . . In this context it does seem quite legitimate, and desirable in the interests of the profession, for information gained through the process of appraisal to be taken into account.

What, one wonders, is the boundary between *direct* and *indirect* in the vocabulary of government?

The relevant paragraph in the supplementary guidance (para 50) appears to confirm the minister's statement:

> In advising governing bodies on decisions about the promotion of teachers, or about the use of their discretion in relation to pay, headteachers should take account of any relevant information deriving from appraisal, along with other factors.

It is difficult to see how the outcomes of appraisal interviews can be used in this way without the intrusion of judgmental factors. We share with the professional organisations and with teachers generally a profound alarm that the Secretary of State appears not to have understood the dangers inherent in using an appraisal system devised with aims totally concerned with personal, professional and institutional improvement (NF para 2) for another, alien purpose.

Nor is the profession's concern confined to matters of pay and promotion. There is a growing fear that, with this as a precedent, in situations where schools have to lose staff, either because of falling rolls or because of budgetary constraints, governors may very well address themselves to the issue by asking the headteacher: 'As a consequence of your recent appraisals, which member of staff would you be most prepared to see go?' This is not a question which headteachers would be able to answer and at the same time maintain the confidence and loyalty of their staff.

SMALL PRIMARY SCHOOLS

Out of a total of over twenty-one thousand primary schools in England and Wales, 22 per cent have one hundred or fewer pupils, according to the 1988 education statistics (TES, 1990b). For Wales this figure is over 36 per cent. With most of these headteachers having a full teaching load, already battling valiantly to manage the many demands of the National Curriculum, it is difficult to see how they can make time to visit the classes of their assistant teachers, let alone conduct a full-scale appraisal. It is widely held that preparation for appraisal requires a total of four days' training in all, with some opportunity for in-school trialling in addition.

A number of LEAs are already grouping small primary schools in consortia, so that expertise in subject areas of the National Curriculum can be shared: Cornwall and Northumberland are two such authorities. This would seem the only reasonable way forward for appraisal too. Five such schools might well muster about eight assistant staff for whose appraisal two of the headteachers in the consortium might by agreement become the trained appraisers. There is no reason why these two might not also undertake the peer appraisal of their colleagues in the consortium, together with the local adviser.

For this there must be, as for all schools, an allowance of time. How much time it is difficult to estimate, other than to say that it must be proportionately more than for larger schools, since there are often considerable distances between schools in the same cluster. A bold move by at least one LEA is to provide each cluster with one support teacher, to use as the schools judge best. This enables schools to vary the use of that teacher according to the demands of the moment: to substitute for a teacher on in-service training, to allow teachers time to see the work of other colleagues, to give time for reading and preparation. Since the demands of appraisal are irregular through the year, it would not be unreasonable if this became an added demand on support time. However, such an LEA is exceptional and, indeed, there is no guarantee as education budgets are slashed that it will be able to maintain this additional staffing. It is even more unlikely, then, that others will be able easily to follow suit.

Those small schools which can be merged have undoubtedly already been reorganised, often to the dismay of those parents who now see their children travelling by bus to another village, away from the community in which primary-age children should most certainly be educated. The arguments of economy wear thin against sound educational practice. Teachers of small schools are often expert copers, remedying their own deficiencies in many ways, some of them highly informal. The National Association for the Support of Small Schools argues convincingly that, given more ancillary and teaching help, these schools will manage as well as their larger brethren. It is vital that that help extends to appraisal.

COMMUNITY SCHOOLS

We have for most of our professional lives taught in or been involved with community schools. It never ceases to amaze us what scant attention these complex organisations receive when any innovatory management issue is under consideration. The Taylor Report (DES, 1977), while making excellent recommendations, by and large now implemented, for the representation of parents and the local community on the governing bodies of schools, has little to say specifically about the governance of community schools. There are now over 750 community schools, both primary and secondary, in well over half the LEAs in England and Wales. Within them are a number of teachers with the title and status of community vice-principal (in Leicestershire), head of department (community), community tutor and the like, who may have some teaching commitment, but whose main role is to take responsibility for the management of community education.

Serious consideration needs to be given as to how these teachers will be appraised. Flexibility and spontaneity, matching community needs with community and professional skills, negotiating, mediating and arbitrating between group and group and between potential activities and resources, are all managerial skills that do not lend themselves easily to standard accountability procedures. If there are reliable performance indicators, we have not come across them.

In some schools these managers operate almost independently of the institution in which they work, even to the extent that there are separate rooms and resources for school and community use. In most, even in a climate of overload and constraints, their work is intrinsic to the philosophy of the institution and the managerial approach is therefore holistic. We see no way in which these community education managers can be reasonably appraised other than by the headteacher and the community education adviser jointly. Whether the adviser has the same role of acting as data collector as in the appraisal of headteachers or has a more proactive role is for the LEA to decide, though we would think the latter is likely to be the more effective, since there is usually a strong working relationship between the community educator and the adviser. Community education resources are generally provided quite distinctly from those for the school, even though the distinction may be blurred in use, and the community manager is accountable directly to the LEA for them.

For goalsetting, it would seem essential that the adviser is a full participant. Whereas in mainstream schools it is only necessary to integrate individual goals with whole school policy, here it is vital that there is also integration with the LEA community education policy. Where there is shared accountability, there must surely also be shared involvement in establishing goals.

In 'fully fledged' community schools, those where many staff both teach in the school and have a community education role, it is important that this second role, even though it may be subsidiary, is also appraised. Many such teachers invest a great deal of energy and display considerable ingenuity in planning their contributions and it is only right that this should be fully recognised and valued. It may be that the appraiser of these teachers has no involvement in community activities and therefore no firsthand knowledge of the past performance and future potentialities in this sphere of the teacher being appraised. It does not seem unreasonable, therefore, that there should also be an independent appraisal discussion with the manager of community education, the outcome of which should be included in the final appraisal report.

CONCLUSION

Provided our national focus is clearly on the improvement of individual and corporate performance for the benefit of the students in our schools, we do not see appraisal as a threat but rather as a means to an end that central government, local government and schools can hold in common. For appraisal to succeed, however, there must be adequate funding, for initial and ongoing training and for its implementation. If the NSG and HMI independent estimates of the annual costs are not met when appraisal becomes fully operational, then appraisal will fail, for there is no such thing as appraisal on the cheap. Just as the devolution to LEAs of in-service training funding, and their consequent ability to relate more directly to school requirements, have disclosed an increased need for funding, so will teacher appraisal. Whatever the other demands that are being made on the national exchequer, education deserves pride of place, since our children are the seed corn of the future.

Appendix 1

Guidance and code of practice on the collection of information for teacher and headteacher appraisal

1 This guidance and Code of Practice covers the collection of information for teacher and headteacher appraisal other than through classroom observation.

GENERAL PRINCIPLES

2 Information collection for the purpose of the appraisal of a teacher or headteacher should be designed to assist discussion in an appraisal interview having the purposes set out in the National Framework.

3 Where it has been agreed that the appraisal should concentrate on specific aspects of the appraisee's job, information collection should likewise concentrate on those aspects.

4 Appraisers should act with sensitivity to all concerned and should not exhibit any bias in collecting information.

5 Those giving information should not be put under any pressure save that of relevance and accuracy.

6 General comments should be supported by specific examples.

7 Interviews for the purpose of information collection should be held on a one-to-one basis.

8 Any information received anonymously should not be used.

9 Information which does not relate to the professional performance of a teacher or headteacher should not be sought or accepted.

10 Appraisees should not adopt an obstructive attitude to reasonable proposals for the collection of appropriate information.

11 Neither appraisers nor appraisees should act in any way that is likely to threaten the trust and confidence on both sides upon which successful appraisal depends.

BACKGROUND INFORMATION

Teacher appraisal

12   The teacher's appraiser must be familiar with relevant national and LEA policies and requirements.

13   The appraiser will also need to acquire a range of background information appropriate to the appraisee's wider professional responsibilities, e.g. the school's statements of aims and objectives, pastoral arrangements, equal opportunities policies, or departmental policies.

14   The appraiser should obtain copies of the teacher's job description.

Headteacher appraisal

15   The headteacher's appraisers must be familiar with current national and (as appropriate) LEA policies and requirements with regard to curriculum, special needs, equal opportunities, staffing and cover, disciplinary and grievance procedures and other such matters relating to school management.

16   They will also need a wide range of background information about the school and its context including:

- curricular policies
- general organisation and deployment of staff
- composition and organisation of the governing body
- links with home, outside bodies and other schools
- the pattern of meetings with staff and with parents
- school activities and routines, including assessment and recording systems, examination results, calendar of events
- staff appraisal and development arrangements and arrangements for induction and probation
- financial and management systems

This information will need to be assembled by appraisee heads, who may provide any supplementary information they wish.

17   The appraisers should obtain copies of the headteacher's job description.

OTHER GUIDANCE TO THE APPRAISER

18   The appraiser should agree with the appraisee at the initial meeting what information it would be appropriate to collect for the purpose of the appraisal, from what sources and by what methods.

19   When interviewing people providing information as part of an appraisal, the appraiser should explain the purpose of the interview

and the way in which information will be treated.

20 Those giving information should be encouraged to make fair and considered comments which they are prepared to acknowledge and to substantiate if required.

21 Any written submissions should remain confidential to the author, the appraiser and the appraisee.

22 Those offering significantly critical comments should be asked to discuss them directly with the appraisee before they are used as appraisal information. (The substance of grievance or disciplinary proceedings should never be used in the appraisal process.)

23 Except where personal opinion is specifically sought (for example where an appraiser is attempting to gauge staff reactions to a particular innovation), care should be taken to ensure that information is sought and presented in an objective way.

Reproduced from: *School Teacher Appraisal:*
The National Framework, DES (1990b)

Appendix 2

Training videos

FOCUS IN EDUCATION, 65 High Street, Hampton Hill, Mddx TW12 1NH

Focus in Education has produced excellent, highly professional videos on behalf of four out of the six pilot projects. Each video is accompanied by a booklet outlining its intent and purpose and giving the running time of each section. In their training workshops the authors have used, and found particularly valuable, the following:

Awareness raising

'Working Together' (Newcastle-upon-Tyne) tape 1, part 1: an 18 minute sequence. Tape 2 has a similar concern in negotiations about classroom observation.

Classroom observation

'Working Together' tape 3: primary PE lesson, 48 minutes; tape 4: secondary Year 9 history lesson, focusing on the dynamics of group discussion, 52 minutes.

'Let's get it Right' (Somerset) tape 1, part 2: primary sequence: briefing session, 7 minutes; lesson, edited to 13 minutes; a very thorough debriefing, with flashbacks to events in the lesson, 15 minutes. Tape 2: secondary English lesson, focusing on group discussion.

'What's in it for Me?' (Suffolk) tape 2: primary mathematics lesson with 6-year-olds; whole lesson followed by discussion, 57 minutes. Tape 3: secondary Year 10 geography; whole lesson followed by discussion, 57 minutes.

Appraisal discussions

'Opening Doors' (Cumbria) tape 2: appraisal of primary deputy head, 56 minutes.

'Let's get it Right' tape 3 (primary), tape 4 (secondary): headteacher appraisal, 48 minutes and 59 minutes respectively.

OPEN UNIVERSITY EDUCATIONAL ENTERPRISES,
12 Cofferidge Close, Stony Stratford, Milton Keynes, MK11 1BY

The Appraisal Interview (E324/08V)

LEAP MANAGEMENT IN EDUCATION

Produced at the BBC's Open University Production Centre and obtainable from LEAs.

Module 2: *Managing staff development* and module 5: *Accountability*. Both provide useful background for appraisal. Videos are included in the module materials.

References

ACAS (1986) *Report of the Appraisal/Training Working Group*, reprinted in HMSO (1989).

AMMA (1988) *Teacher Appraisal: Problems and Practicalities*, AMMA Education Conference Report, London: AMMA.

Arkin, A. (1989) 'AMMA softens its advice on appraisal scheme boycott', *Times Educational Supplement*, 17 November 1989.

Barnard, C.I. (1938) *The Functions of the Executive*, Cambridge, Mass: Harvard University Press.

Bayter, J.A. (1989) 'Approaches to Staff Appraisal in British Polytechnic Libraries', unpublished M.Lib. thesis, University College of Wales.

Beare, H., Millikan, R. and Caldwell, B. (1989) *Creating an Excellent School*, London: Routledge.

Bell, L. (ed.) (1988) *Appraising Teachers in Schools*, London: Routledge.

Boud, D.J. and Turner, C.J. (1974) 'A method for the evaluation of a traditional lecture course' in *Research into Tertiary Science Education*, a selection of papers from the Conference on Tertiary Science Education, December 1972, Society for Research into Higher Education.

Bunnell, S. and Stephens, E. (1984) 'Teacher appraisal: a democratic approach', *School Organisation* 4(4).

Burns, T. and Stalker, G.M. (1968) *The Management of Innovation*, London: Tavistock.

Darling-Hammond, L., Wise, A.E. and Pease, S.R. (1983) 'Teacher evaluation in the organizational context: a review of the literature', *Review of Educational Research* 53 (3).

Dennison, W.F. and Shenton, K. (1987) *Challenges in Educational Management*, London: Routledge.

DES (1977) *A New Partnership for our Schools* (The Taylor Report), London: HMSO.

DES (1983) *Teaching Quality*, London: HMSO.

DES (1986) *Education (No.2) Act*, London: HMSO.

DES (1986) *Better Schools: Evaluation and Appraisal Conference*, London: HMSO.

DES (1988) *Education Reform Act*, London: HMSO.

DES (1989a) Circular letter 'Report of the National Steering Group and the Government's Response', 2 October 1989.

DES (1989b) HMI Report *Developments in the Appraisal of Teachers*, London: Department of Education and Science.

DES (1990a) *Planning for School Development*, London: DES.

DES (1990b) draft of *School Teacher Appraisal: The National Framework*, London: DES.

Evertson, C.M. and Holley, F.M. (1981) 'Classroom observation' in J. Millman (ed.) *Handbook of Teacher Evaluation*, Beverley Hills, Calif.: Sage Publications.

Gane, V. (1986) *Secondary Headteacher Appraisal: The Nub of Credibility*, Bristol: National Development Centre for School Management Training.

Gromisch, D.S. (1972) 'A comparison of student and departmental chairmen's evaluations of teaching performance, *Journal of Medical Education*, 47.

Hall, V., Morgan, C. and Mackay, H. (1985) 'Defining headship – an impossible task?' London: Secondary Heads' Association Review.

Hall, V., Mackay, H. and Morgan C. (1986) *The Teacher at Work*, Milton Keynes: Open University Press.

Hellawell, D. (1990) 'Headteacher appraisal: relationships with the LEA and its inspectorate', *Educational Management and Administration* 18 (1).

Herzberg, F.W. (1966) *Work and the Nature of Man*, London: Staples Press.

Heywood, J. (1989) 'Agenda', *Guardian*, 24 October.

HMI (1985a) *Education Observed 3: Good Teachers*, London: DES.

HMI (1985b) *Quality in Schools: Evaluation and Appraisal*, London: HMSO.

HMSO (1989) *School Teacher Appraisal: A National Framework*, London: HMSO.

Hord, S. (1987) *Evaluating Educational Innovation*, London: Croom Helm.

Hughes, M. (1976) 'The professional as administrator: the case of the secondary school head' in R.S. Peters (1976).

IAC (1990) *Third Report of the Interim Advisory Committee on School Teachers' Pay and Conditions*, London: DES.

Joseph, K. (1984) *Speech to the North of England Education Conference*, January 1984, London: DES.

Knapp, M.S. (1982) *Toward the study of teacher evaluation as an organizational process*, Menlo Park, Calif.: Educational and Human Resources Research Center.

Leonard, M. (1988) *The 1988 Education Act: A Tactical Guide for Schools*, Oxford: Blackwell.

Lewin, K. (1947) 'Frontiers in group dynamics: method and reality in social sciences; social equilibria and social change', *Human Relations* 1(1).

Lovington District (1988) 'Lovington Public Schools: Teaching Competencies', Lovington, New Mexico: Board of Education.

Lyons, G. (1974) *The Administrative Tasks of Head and Senior Teachers in Large Secondary Schools*, Bristol: University of Bristol.

McGregor, D.G. (1960) *The Human Side of Enterprise*, London: McGraw-Hill.

MacGregor, J. (1990a) 'Speech to the North of England Education Conference', *Times Educational Supplement*, 12 January.

MacGregor, J. (1990b) 'Appraisal', in *Head Teachers Review* (Winter 1989/90), London: NAHT.

MacGregor, J. (1990c) *Speech to the BEMAS Conference*, September, London: DES.

McMahon, A., Bolam, R., Abbott, R. and Holly, P. (1984) *Guidelines for Review and Internal Development in Schools*, York: Longman.

Maslow, A.H. (1959) *Motivation and Human Personality*, New York: Harper.

Mintzberg, H. (1979) *The Structuring of Organizations*, Englewood Cliffs, NJ: Prentice-Hall.

Montgomery, D. (1985) 'Teacher appraisal: a theory and practice for evaluation and enhancement', *Inspection and Advice* 21(1).

Moran, M. (1990) 'Appraisal in a Cumbrian secondary school', in *Head Teachers Review* (Winter 1989/90), London: NAHT.

Morgan, C., Hall, V. and Mackay, H. (1983) *The Selection of Secondary Headteachers*, Milton Keynes: Open University Press.

NDC (1988) *Consortium of School Teacher Appraisal Pilot Schemes; Progress on Appraisal: an interim report*, Bristol: National Development Centre for School Management Training.

Newman, J. (1985) *Staff Appraisal Schemes in the South Midlands and the South West*, York: Centre for the Study of Comprehensive Schools.

Nottinghamshire LEA (1985) *Teacher Professional Appraisal as part of a Development Programme*, Nottingham: Nottinghamshire LEA.

NUT (1981) *A Fair Way Forward: NUT Memorandum on Appointment, Promotion and Career Development*, London: NUT.

NUT (1985) *Teacher Appraisal and Teaching Quality: An NUT Policy Statement*, London: NUT.

Oklahoma (1989) *Minimum Criteria for Effective Teaching and Administrative Performance*, Oklahoma City, Ok: Oklahoma State Department of Education.

Peters, T.J. and Waterman, R.H. (1982) *In Search of Excellence: Lessons from America's Best-run Companies*, London: Harper & Row.

Peters, R.S. (ed.) (1976) *The Role of the Head*, London: Routledge & Kegan Paul.

Pilley, J. and Poster, C. (1988) *Inservice Education and Training in the South West: A Survey Undertaken on Behalf of the Manpower Services Commission*, Bristol: National Development Centre for School Management Training.

Poster, C. D. (1976) *School Decision Making*, London: Heinemann.

Ramsden, P. (1975) 'Polytechnic students' expectations of their teachers, and the use of a student feedback questionnaire', *Higher Education Bulletin* 3(2).

Randall, G., Packard, P. and Slater, J. (1984) *Staff Appraisal: A First Step to Effective Leadership*, London: Institute of Personnel Management.

Richardson, E. (1973) *The Teacher, the School and the Task of Management*, London: Heinemann.

Robson, M. (ed.) (1984) *Quality Circles in Action*, Aldershot: Gower.

Sagan, H.B. (1974) 'Student faculty and departmental chairmen ratings of instructors: who agrees with whom?' *Research in Higher Education* 2(3).

Sallis, J. (1988) *Schools, Parents and Governors*, London: Routledge.

Suffolk LEA (1985) *Those Having Torches*, Ipswich: Suffolk Education Department.

TES (1989a) 'Merger of minds', *Times Educational Supplement*, 13 October.

TES (1989b) 'NASUWT statement', *Times Educational Supplement*, 17 November.

TES (1990a) 'Appraisal – pay link denied', *Times Educational Supplement*, 2 February.

TES (1990b) 'Tiny worlds forgotten by a big-time operator' *Times Educational Supplement*, 9 February.

Texas (1988) *Teacher Appraisal System*, Vol. 1, *Teacher Orientation Manual*, Vol. 2, *Appraiser's Manual*, Austin, Tx: Texas Education Agency.

Trethowan, D. (1987) *Appraisal and Target Setting*, London: Harper & Row.

Turner, C.M. (1981) *Appraisal Systems*, Coombe Lodge working paper, Blagdon: Further Education Staff College.

Turner, G. and Clift, P. (1985) *A First Review and Register of School and College Based Teacher Appraisal Schemes*, Milton Keynes: Open University Press.

Vroom, V.H. (1964) *Work and Motivation*, New York: Wiley.

Wallace, M. (1986) *A Directory of School Management Development Activities and Resources*, Bristol: National Development Centre for School Management Training.

Wieck, K.E. (1976) 'Educational organizations as loosely coupled systems', *Administrative Science Quarterly* 21.

Wilkinson, C. and Cave, E. (1988) *Teaching and Managing: Inseparable Activities in Schools*, London: Routledge.

Winkley, D. (1985) *Diplomats and Detectives – the LEA Advisers at Work*, London: Robert Royce.

Wragg, E.C. (1987) *Teacher Appraisal: A Practical Guide*, Basingstoke: Macmillan.

Index